RELIGIOUS ORDERS OF WOMEN

IS VOLUME

86

OF THE

Twentieth Century Encyclopedia of Catholicism

UNDER SECTION

VIII

THE ORGANIZATION OF THE CHURCH

IT IS ALSO THE

123RD

VOLUME IN ORDER OF PUBLICATION

Edited by HENRI DANIEL-ROPS of the Académie Française

"It is not to amuse you that I have loved you," Christ reminded the nun, St. Angela of Foligno. His words indicate the response and the sacrifice that Christ requires from those engaged in the religious life. Reflecting this response and sacrifice are the one million Catholic women who, as members of religious orders, have forever renounced the secular life.

What are the motives that draw a woman to this arduous form of life? Suzanne Cita-Malard shows how the religious life for women can in many ways be a satisfying as well as a sanctifying achievement. Women religious, she explains, are able to gain a goodly measure of spiritual happiness by persevering in their lives of poverty, chastity and obedience.

Beginning with an overall picture of the religious vocation, the author describes how the nun tries to cultivate virtue in her continual search for sancity. Writing briefly and clearly, she outlines the history and developments of the sisterhoods since their beginnings in the second century.

The customs, the requirements and the work of the first groups are compared with those of today, and both the similarities and the differences of each era reveal the continuity and adaptability of the orders. The traditional con-

:he habit, the different
—all these aspects and
at length.
re the chapters dealing
e forms of the sacred
:r led by the many con-
ıching nuns, the nurses,
ered orders and women
Institutes are all care-
ɔractical and spiritual

g the reader up to date
ıs of various commu-
ı in the modern world
:ance of the Secular In-
: XII. A brief appendix
lescribing the Council
:riors which has been
:ates and Great Britain.
ʼas born in France in
ge granted by the Holy
isit and study religious
countries. In addition,
ɪks including the much-
'. The *Académie Fran-*
:ate to her three times
is well known for the
she has written and
produced in collaboration with her mother.

George J. Robinson translated this work from the original French.

RELIGIOUS ORDERS OF WOMEN

By SUZANNE CITA-MALARD

Translated from the French by GEORGE J. ROBINSON

HAWTHORN BOOKS · PUBLISHERS · *New York*

 This book was manufactured in the United States of America and published simultaneously in Canada by Prentice-Hall of Canada, Ltd., 520 Ellesmere Road, Scarborough, Ontario. It was originally published in France under the title *Un Million de religieuses,* © Librairie Artheme Fayard, 1960. The Library of Congress has catalogued the Twentieth Century Encyclopedia of Catholicism under card number 58-14327. Library of Congress Catalogue Card Number for this volume: 64-14165. The Catholic University of America Library has catalogued this volume based on the Lynn-Peterson Alternative Classification for Catholic Books: BQT184. T9v.86/BQX6841. Suggested decimal classification: 271.9.

First Edition, October, 1964

NIHIL OBSTAT

Joannes M. T. Barton, S.T.D., L.S.S.

Censor Deputatus

IMPRIMATUR

✠ Patritius Casey

Vicarius Generalis

Westmonasterii, die IV JULII MCMLXIV

The Nihil obstat and Imprimatur are a declaration that a book or pamphlet is considered to be free from doctrinal or moral error. It is not implied that those who have granted the Nihil obstat and Imprimatur agree with the contents, opinions, or statements expressed.

H-9523

CONTENTS

INTRODUCTION

In his book on religious Orders of men in this series, Professor Jean Canu sketched out the historical stages in the development of the consecrated life of religious, beginning with the purely monastic phase and then going on to the religious life present and working in the world. Scholarly and to the point as his synopsis is, it did not entirely release us from the obligation of charting the evolution of religious women through the centuries, though it does do away with the need for a long and historical study on the subject. As we study the religious life led by women in these times, we shall see that, side by side with the older forms which have been more or less adapted to modern circumstances, new approaches have sprung up encouraged by the Holy See for their apostolic vitality.

Most religious men, whether priests or not, in one way or another are teachers. For religious women, on the other hand, whether they teach or are contemplative only, the religious life is a ministry of charity or, to be more precise, charity incarnate. If there seems to be an infinite number of Orders and Congregations of religious women, it is because there is more bodily and spiritual suffering to assuage than there are truths to teach or errors to refute. Love's initiatives are far less limited than the data of consciousness. Men work out programmes of operations, and women put them into practical application. During the time a man spends working out his programme, a woman will tackle the job at hand with the best practical method, which may often be changed or adapted to suit pressing needs more closely and immediately. In his rôle of sacramental sanctifier, the priest fulfils the work of Christ.

Chaste and maternal like the Blessed Virgin, the nun is another Mary, which is why she makes her own the words of Mary at the Annunciation: "Behold the handmaid of the Lord."

As in the previous volume in this series dealing with the religious life for men the term religious Order, in the title, has been used in the popular sense, that is, as applying to all associations of religious women under vows, whether they are Orders or Congregations. In the technical sense religious Order should be used only of those institutes in which solemn vows are taken and whose members, again in the technical sense, are nuns; others, who take simple vows, are, properly speaking, members of a Congregation and should be known as sisters. On the difference between simple and solemn vows see, in this series, *What is Canon Law?* by René Metz, pp. 88–9.

It would be impossible in a book of this nature even to enumerate all the Orders and Congregations of women religious—the list in the *Annuario Pontificio* (1964) runs to just over 100 pages and mentions 1,144 institutions, some 440 of which are represented in Great Britain and the United States.

CHAPTER I

WHAT IS A NUN?

Only God knows exactly how many women have given up marriage for his service. We do know, however, that the Church officially records a million religious women, at present listed as members of religious Orders or Congregations, or Secular Institutes.

Besides these—and we should note this fact at the outset of this study—there have been for several centuries, and continue to be, religious women who are not Catholics. Though their aspirations, way of life and motivation may all have been different, it is nonetheless striking that every age, every latitude, every rite and religious belief have all had women so conscious of God's transcendence that they have consecrated their lives to his service.

The religious life, then, is not an invention of Catholicism. Nevertheless, the Incarnation of God's Word in the womb of the Virgin Mary and his Real Presence among us in the Eucharist have given a wider meaning to the life of consecrated women. That is why our epoch has seen entire communities of Protestant deaconesses and sisters become Catholics, and Buddhist nuns becoming Cistercian nuns. Their search for the Absolute has brought them from the hinterlands of faith right to the centre, which a woman's heart recognizes more easily as Love.

Surely there is matter for thought and reflection in the paradox that, out of more than three thousand millions in the whole world, and about five hundred million Catholics, a million women have renounced for ever the legitimate pleasures and needs of the body—most often without ever having known them—and have stripped themselves of everything, even their wills, to bind themselves to a public fulfilment of the strict and detailed obligations of a rule imposing community life on them, or to dedicate themselves to an apostolate, while remaining in the world and at their professions, which, though it is more or less hidden, makes their lives nonetheless a complete oblation. Their commitments and obligations are, of course, diametrically opposed to the freedom claimed by our independent, selfish and pleasure-seeking era.

There are even more than a million if, to the statistics provided by the Sacred Congregation for Religious, which lists eight hundred thousand canonically recognized women religious, we add the members of the new associations whose diffusion Pius XII was the first to encourage, just as he was the first to organize their very flexible structure, which adapts itself to all social circumstances and individual possibilities.

Secular Institutes are discussed later. For the moment we can see what is the religious state properly speaking. Canon 487 says that the religious life is "the communal and stable manner of living wherein the faithful, in addition to the precepts common to all, bind themselves to observe the evangelical counsels as well, through the vows of obedience, chastity and poverty".

An imitation on this earth of the Jerusalem above, and therefore free of the encumbrance of the three concupiscences, this state, according to Christian tradition, is the anticipation in this life of the kingdom of heaven. The religious life, whose members are "witnesses of the City of God", is, therefore, a state of tending to perfection within a community of charity and adoration.

But is it tending only? This is exactly the point some modern Christians miss when they see that some religious—and particularly women religious, who are the special object of their lack of understanding and, frequently, of their ironical remarks—have their own idiosyncrasies or even human faults, be they serious or not. The thing to remember is that, because a human being has entered into a state of perfection, she has not suddenly lost the ability to sin. On the contrary, a sister who considered herself better than a wife and mother, or a spinster, would be guilty of pride. Situated as she is, at least in theory, in an atmosphere which is more favourable than any secular state to the cultivation of virtue and the search for sanctity, the fact is that a woman religious is more blameworthy than others if she becomes bogged down in routine or mediocrity, succumbs to temptation—which not even the most cloistered convent can keep out—or misses, by however little, her mark which is to be the leaven in the dough. But make no mistake about it: to be, and to remain, a good religious demands uncommon courage: "It is not to amuse you that I have loved you," our Lord reminded St Angela of Foligno. This famous remark highlights two aspects of the religious life: it is a response, and it is a sacrifice.

It can, of course, be only a creature's response to a preference already implanted by her Creator, since no being can pride itself on having loved God before having been loved by him. And he loves all of us, religious or lay people, believers or not—but not all in the same way. When God draws a soul to the religious life, it is to mark it with the seal of his special love.

Common theological opinion today is that a soul is free to accept or refuse this divine invitation. And perhaps someone would consider it downright foolish to evade such a flattering invitation from the King of kings. But if it is flattering, it is also demanding, and there are thousands of girls who have been thus "foolish", certain of whom consider themselves wise in the way of the world. Different from a spurned human suitor, our Lord does not nurse a grudge against a girl who has preferred a human husband to himself, and preferred the free exercise of her paltry human liberties. This Master is no tyrant, and he respects our free will. But it will be a sad awakening to find out, in heaven, that one has renounced a rare opportunity to spend one's life with Love itself.

The will to strive for perfection in the religious life, which comes down to living the Gospel to the full by imitating the angels in complete self-abnegation, is merely an illusion if it does not correspond to God's will and to his gratuitous offer which is usually made to an innocent soul, but sometimes lifts to the heights one that has strayed.

But we must be careful here, too. Anyone who is aspiring to the "life of perfection" and realizes, or whose superiors point out, that he or she is not made for that life, is not necessarily a defeated candidate for sanctity. We may remember M. and Mme Martin, the parents of St Teresa of Lisieux, neither of whom was able to enter the cloister. In their case, which was exceptional of course, a religious vocation passed them by (their cause for beatification has been opened) to work in the souls of their children.

By no means should a religious vocation be considered as a purely individual phenomenon, but rather as a nominative grace included in the appeal to the human race, an appeal which originates with our forefathers and is frequently the culmination of a centuries old endeavour (an example of this is the prayer, which was immediately answered, of St Teresa at her clothing: "If Léonie [her sister] has no vocation, give it to her").

A vocation is a gift of God to humanity as well as to the person to whom he gives it. It is, consequently, important to stress the point that, though she may be especially loved in herself by him who has called her, a woman religious is also "seen by God in his people".

CHAPTER II

THE DEVELOPMENT OF RELIGIOUS LIFE FOR WOMEN

The custom of consecrating virgins and giving them the veil existed as long ago as the second century. In Gaul and Africa, the *velatio* could take place in a woman's twenty-fifth year, but in Spain she had to be at least forty. On the other hand, a dispensation from this age limit could be given in the case of a girl who was precociously virtuous, or because of the bishop's special consideration. Thus, St Geneviève, who had been dedicated to God by St Germanus when she was only seven, was solemnly consecrated, with two companions, by the bishop of Auxerre when she was fifteen. This happened a few years after the Council of Ephesus had proclaimed the virginity and divine maternity of Mary. After the Council, reflection on this twofold mystery had generated countless vocations.

In addition to the consecrated virgins, there were widows who were called deaconesses—a title conferred by a special blessing given them by the bishop—and led a life of almsgiving and sheltering the homeless and the traveller. The consecrated virgins were contemplatives, while the widows led an "active" life.

At first, consecrated virgins remained in their family homes.

St Athanasius' visit to a widow, Albina, whose daughter, Marcella, had only been married for seven months and slept on a rough pallet, resulted in the foundation on the Aventine hill in Rome of a community of virgins and widows who lived a life of prayer and austerity and whose superior was Marcella. It was for one of this community, Marcellina, that St Ambrose wrote his *De virginitate.* St Eustochium, St Paula's daughter, helped her mother to establish two convents in Bethlehem, and it was to her that St Jerome dedicated his well-known letters on virginity. (Among the Hieronymites, who still have foundations in Spain, and whose convents are distinguished for their love of Scripture and their special attention to fraternal charity, St Eustochium is the patron of novices.)

Gradually, the solemn consecration of virgins living alone—which was often imperilled by the widespread paganism of society at the time—was replaced by the vows of chastity, poverty and obedience, the two latter signifying, with the surrender of all personal goods, life in a community under the government of a superior who personified the divine will. Enclosure, which was introduced to protect nuns against the barbarian invasions, was established in its absolute form by Boniface VIII's decree, *Periculoso*, in 1283. Thus, not only monasticism, properly so called, but the entire religious life, whatever its particular form, is built on a commitment which implies these three vows.

The consecration of virgins according to the Roman Pontifical became increasingly infrequent outside convents; since 1927, it is not allowed except in convents which have papal enclosure for whom Pius XI allowed it to be revived in favour of those who fulfilled the necessary conditions. The reasons for this are quite easy to understand: if the Church is to take such solemn responsibility for an individual's virginity, then that virginity must obviously be protected and be above all suspicion. Besides, this distinction may be better earned by complete detachment from one's own goods and absolute submission to a rule of life which removes the possibility of handling one's own affairs. No matter how greatly an individual nature may be transformed by grace, it will find these two restrictions more burdensome than the control of the senses voluntarily assumed for love of the Infinite and Pure Being.

The cornerstones of monasticism were laid at the beginning of the fourth century by St Antony, then by St Pachomius, who was the first to legislate for community life, and by St Basil. In the next century, St Augustine, St Benedict and St Caesarius all drew up their rules. At the same time, side by side with the monasteries for men established by these giants of the ascetical life, St Pachomius's sister, then St Benedict's—the gentle Scholastica, to whom a providential night of storm brought such renown—opened houses of learning and work where women lived according to a rule modified to suit their needs and the abilities of their sex. They were followed in these foundations by many others, among whom were those widowed or repudiated queens: Bathilde at Chelles, Radegund at Poitiers, Joan at Bourges and Bridget in Sweden, who made available to women havens of culture and work in which, discreetly adapted to their condition, the practice of the Rule was initiated.

More than fifteen centuries of constant use have not affected the enduring strength of the formulas of sanctity drawn up by Basil, Augustine, Benedict and by Bernard of Clairvaux who, six hundred years after the death of the patriarch of the West, was to become his most illustrious descendant; it is no exaggeration to credit him with the rapid development of the Cistercian Benedictines, founded by Robert of Molesmes and Stephen Harding. Even nowadays there are modern Secular Institutes in existence who look to these centuries-old rules for their inspiration.

The spiritual daughters of St Caesarius were adopted by the monks of St Bruno, who preceded St Bernard by a short time and whose rule was an immeasurable boon to the eremitical life, and became Carthusian nuns. Elias, whom the religious of Carmel claim as their father, had to wait, on the other hand, until the end of the fifteenth century before he could look down from heaven on the growing number of young women affiliating themselves to his order under the generalship of John Soreth. Among the first of these were English anchoresses, who were attracted by Carmel's eremitical ideal, Flemish *béguines*, and Spanish *beatas*, all of whom had already had some previous experience of the ascetical life. During the next century, St Mary Magdalen dei Pazzi, without revolutionary change, was to lead her Italian sisters towards "pure contemplation", the end and purpose of the Carmelite order. This revolution—now called the Reform of Carmel—was effected by Teresa de Ahumada, born in Avila in the same year that Mary Magdalen dei Pazzi entered the convent, who carried out her task with a spirit of genius at once completely realistic and absorbed in God.

Anchoresses were consecrated virgins who received episcopal permission to be solemnly enclosed within a small cell; their spiritual and physical nourishment was passed to them through a grating, and consisted of the Eucharist and whatever food the local people provided as alms. St Colette of Corbie, who had been an anchoress, was led to leave her cell, in which she had resolved to remain until death, to reform the Poor Ladies, or Poor Clares, many of whom, since then, have been known as "Colettines".

In the twelfth century, Dominic de Guzman and Francis of Assisi appeared on the scene. Their spiritual daughters, the Dominican nuns and the Poor Clares, were to remain in their cloisters making fruitful the wandering apostolate of the conqueror of the Cathari and the Poor Man of Assisi by their contemplation and mortification. After a while, Third Orders arose from the "Mendicant Orders", a term which was shortly to be applied to the Friars Preachers and the Friars Minor, as well as to the Augustinians, the Carmelites, the Mercedarians, Trinitarians, Servites, Hieronymites and

Minims, all of whom had "Second Orders" of nuns under their care.

The principal purpose of the Third Orders, open to lay people, most of them married, was not only to assist each member in his own sanctification, but to rechristianize a society about to be infected by the paganism of the Renaissance. They were, then, "Catholic Action" groups, long before the term came into use, and had for their field of apostolate their own station in life—an apostolate which is not, clearly, a twentieth-century idea. It was not surprising, of course, that vocations to the religious life should be felt among the members of these fraternities who led a life of fervent prayer and mortification according to a rule binding them to live simply and without luxury in their homes, and to aid one another, give alms, and visit the sick and imprisoned according to each one's situation, ability and means.

Examples of religious, though not formally "monastic", vocations are St Catherine of Siena, St Rose of Lima, St Anne Maria de Paredes (known as the "Rose of Quito"), the very young St Rose of Viterbo. All of them recalled, after ten centuries, the example of St Bridget of Kildare, who at the court of the kings of Ireland accompanied herself on her harp while singing of the life and miracles of St Patrick. The Sisters of Penance of the Third Order of St Dominic all continued to live in their family homes while under private vows. It was the custom then that they might wear the habit of their Order, without which—an important fact to be kept in mind—they would have been without influence and prestige among their neighbours. Sometimes, young disciples gathered round them, forming small communities which were the beginnings of the Third Orders regular. This "halfway house" between the cloister and the world gave the most capable of them possibilities, opportunities and missions of extreme importance. Some of them became the admonitors of popes and the counsellors of princes without causing any stir among ordinary lay people—whom they also frequently exhorted to a better life. Surely St Vincent de Paul had forgotten about these great women, who had been given personal mandates by God, when he said—as we shall recall later—that women had been deprived of any public rôle in the Church for eight centuries.

Naturally, all of these people were not saints, and it was inevitable that the rapid growth of these groups should bring abuse in its wake. But abuse began in the monasteries themselves, where enclosure had been relaxed and the parlours crowded with visiting lay people. These visits were more tolerated—perhaps more complacently encouraged—in convents, where there were many young women who had obeyed, not the call of a vocation, but the expectations of their parents or the conventions of contemporary society. But the Council of Trent reacted strongly in the middle of the sixteenth century, decreeing that all pious women living in community should become nuns, take solemn vows and, thereby, be subject to the rule of enclosure.

But what did that mean? That every woman, whether she was unmarried or a widow, who wished to make public profession of her dedication to the Lord must be enclosed? Precisely. And the only choice she had was among the various enclosed convents.

Laws are made to be interpreted, and ecclesiastical law, when it is strictly disciplinary and does not touch on dogma or morality, may also be adapted. Besides, St Paul says that there is no law which militates against the fruits of the Holy Spirit, which he lists in the Epistle to the Galatians as charity, joy, peace, patience, benignity, goodness, longanimity, mildness, faith, modesty, continency and chastity. But this sounds very much like the qualities of a good hospital nun. Of course, the fact that she would remain a laywoman, though she did make private vows, did not keep a woman determined to "crucify to Christ her flesh, her passions and her longings" from living in community with other sisters also dedicated to the spiritual and corporal works of mercy. For that matter, not even community life was indispensable. St Angela Merici solved this problem at the time of the Council of Trent with her first confraternity of young women which she placed under the patronage of St Ursula. But we shall return to St Angela's solution, after examining how the works of mercy were carried out in the West after the disappearance of deaconesses in the sixth century.

We must return to the origins of the religious life. First of all, the guest quarters of religious houses, whether they were for men or women, never stopped being refuges for foundlings, schools for the children of the neighbourhood, soup-kitchens for the poor, lodging-houses for pilgrims and hospitals for the wounded and the sick found by good samaritans by the roadside.

In the early centuries of the Church, many dioceses had houses of charity which took in the unfortunate of every kind. St Gregory Nazianzen tells us that, to help the needy, his friend St Basil, then still a priest, organized what we should now call a "Catholic Welfare Society" in Cappadocia.

Later, other bishops, and then parish priests, were forced by the hardness of the times and their flocks' needs to establish local groups of volunteers from among their faithful, young people on whose piety and devotion they could count. We shall see later more instances of this method of recruiting helpers in charitable undertakings.

The first foundress of a charity hospital was Fabiola—not Cardinal Wiseman's heroine, but a Roman widow of the tribe of the Fabia—who returned from a pilgrimage to the Holy Land to establish a hospital in Rome.

The Hôtel-Dieu in Paris goes back to the eighth century and has been the prototype of many others. The wise and moderate rule of St Augustine has been the basis for many of the rules adopted by hospital nuns. The Ladies of Charity whom St Vincent de Paul sent to visit these establishments may have found many things needing improvement, but that was because the sisters and other workers in these hospitals were overwhelmed by the number of sick people whom they had either to refuse to admit or—contagiously ill or not—put in a bed with one or more other patients. At Montpellier, on the other hand, the Hospitallers of the Holy Spirit had been instructed by their founder, Guy de Montpellier, to give each of the foundlings left at their door a "single and separate bed, lest they suffer any harm".

Though it was not based on solemn vows, this type of religious life was, obviously, no less ordained by God according to a rule established on the practice of the Gospel counsels.

With the beginnings of feminine emancipation in the sixteenth century, a direct result of the general development of education, women called by God to his service were given the chance to participate in apostolic activity. Some of them, while retaining solemn vows, with the safeguard of a slightly mitigated rule of enclosure, worked in hospitals or as teachers.

One of the first of these groups were the Augustinian Canonesses of the Mercy of Jesus, who were founded at Vannes in France in 1635, and the Sisters of Our Lady of Charity (the "Good Shepherd" nuns), who were founded by St John Eudes and added to the three usual vows a fourth, according to which they bound themselves to zeal for souls and the rehabilitation of fallen women.

In 1597, Blessed Alix Le Clerc, under the direction of St Peter Fourier, founded the Canonesses of St Augustine, for the education of girls. Earlier, in 1536, St Angela Merici had been able to establish a community similar to the one for which Mary Ward had unsuccessfully asked permission: a group of women without public vows, community life or special dress, who would bind themselves to chastity, seclusion from the world and obedience. Eventually, St Charles Borromeo, who was then Archbishop of Milan, gathered some of these early Ursulines into a community. In time, the community spread to France, throughout Italy, to England and America. Each national group developed its own particular customs and practices (some, for instance, made solemn vows and were bound to papal enclosure) but, in 1928, various congregations of Ursulines were joined together to make the Roman Union and adopted a religious habit which combined "the cincture of Paris, the ring of Italy, the headdress of America, the wimple of Angers, the crucifix of Toulouse and the veil of Bordeaux".

St Ignatius Loyola, the founder of the Society of Jesus, who abolished the choral Office for his subjects and was the first to introduce simple vows, apparently exercised only an indirect influence on the religious life for women since neither he nor his successors would agree to the establishment or accept the government of a Congregation of women attached to their Order. But the spirit of St Ignatius, and his constitutions, his Spiritual Exercises, and the solid training given to each Jesuit, all inspired the creation of Congregations of simple vows in the eighteenth and nineteenth centuries. Some of these Congregations are contemplative, such as the Institute of Marie Réparatrice, while others live a "mixed" life, such as the Religious of the Sacred Heart of Jesus, the Religious of the Cenacle, and the Helpers of the Holy Souls. Another group are the Daughters of the Heart of Mary, who were founded during the French Revolution by Fr de Clorivière, S.J., and still retain the privilege of being genuine religious though not bound to community life or the wearing of a religious habit. But we shall return to this group later. Then there are the Daughters of Charity, who, though living in community and wearing a religious habit, part of which is their now famous "winged bonnet", could not in the seventeenth century claim to be religious.

It was charity, or a Pauline "faith working through charity", which led many foundresses to call for adaptation so that their religious could teach the children of the poor. The Daughters of the Cross, who were founded by Madame de Villeneuve with the encouragement of St Francis de Sales, were such a group, as also were the Charitable Sisters of the Holy Infant Jesus, founded in 1682 by a Minim, Fr Nicolas Barré, to teach the children of the middle and lower classes.

Other congregations founded with a similar end were St Frances of Rome's Oblates, and the first congregation of Sisters of St Joseph, those of Puy, and the first Daughters of Providence.

After a while, national upheavals, paradoxically, were to act as an incentive and stimulus to religious groups, whose greatest enemy they often were. Many religious Orders and Congregations were abolished because of the French Revolution, the troubled times of Elizabeth I, Bismarck's *Kulturkampf* and, in our own day, the spread of Soviet domination through the satellite countries behind the Iron Curtain. The one lesson which these catastrophes have consistently taught is that religious Congregations inevitably rise again stronger and more purposeful after having been victimized and, in some cases, decimated by anti-religious forces. Dom Robert Lemoine, O.S.B. says that "the French Revolution may be looked on as one of the causes of the development of Church law.... When religious peace had been restored, the practical inconveniences of solemn vows, still forbidden by civil law, were recognized and simple vows were taken instead."[1]

During the past three centuries, in fact, many religious Congregations of this kind have been founded as a result of political upheavals which, in themselves, had very little to recommend them. In his Constitution, *Conditae a Christo*, Leo XIII made the members of such Congregations real religious by recognizing simple vows; this legislation was later confirmed by Benedict XV's Code of Canon Law.

What justification is there for so large and varied a number of Congregations of simple vows, a class, moreover, approved and encouraged in numbers greater than any other, until the more or less recent appearance of the Secular Institutes? The justification for the variety has always lain in its effects. With these effects in mind, then, it may be well to have a closer look at the religious life for women under its various aspects: contemplative, first of all, it is also missionary, as this vocation

[1] Robert Lemoine, O.S.B., *Le droit des religieux* (Paris, 1956).

includes all the others; later, it developed so that women religious became hospital workers and teachers, living what is now called a "polyvalent" vocation and constantly uncovering new apostolic "specialities". If it now seems that no task is too difficult or strenuous for women religious, it is because the Church now possesses the entire scale of the states of perfection and can so make use of it that all her various needs are met. Nevertheless, poverty, chastity and obedience, explicitly or implicitly vowed or promised, and therefore involving close ties with superiors, remain, even without common life, the fundamental requirements of the religious life. Before proceeding further with our inquiry we must consider the essence of these three vows and also prayer, which is a nun's principal activity.

CHAPTER III

THE ESSENCE AND FORM OF THE VOWS

More than an innate or acquired virtue, chastity is a grace, and this is why its full supernatural meaning is beyond anyone without that grace: "Let him who can understand, understand". And it is for those reasons "which reason knows not of", the heart's reasons, that a young woman dedicates her virginity to our Lord, as a "new tomb, wherein God inters himself".

St Paul encouraged women who were still virgins to remain in that state to "spare them the tribulations of the world". At first glance, this seems almost a mere act of self-defence. On the contrary, as soon as chastity is consecrated to God, it becomes an offering based on the expectation and acceptance of trials, since it is made to imitate more closely him who prophesied his Passion by saying, "And I, being lifted up, will draw all things to myself". Biblical scholars look at St Paul's words in their context and conclude that what he is implying is that married people are encumbered by their bodies in their quest for the one thing necessary. Anything which could keep us away from union with God was a tribulation for St Paul.

Of course, even the most happily married woman always runs the risk of being deserted, beaten or betrayed. Even if she enjoys good health, she may not be able to have children, or, if she can, they may be born sick, die shortly after birth, be mentally defective, or grow up with bad characters. But the point to remember here is that most women who are unhappily married (or who think they are) make their own consolation: they are right, and "he" is in the wrong. In itself, the pleasure some people get from being misunderstood is absurd. For many women, however, it is very pleasant.

But women religious are not allowed the luxury of this shirking of personal responsibilities and the compensation of self-love. Whatever the formal perfection of their state of life, their whole existence means daily and enduring contact between their own imperfection, and the unattainable and infinite holiness of God. And they cannot deny or excuse their unworthiness. Since nothing so disturbs the feminine psychology as much as the certainty of its own inadequacy, the question arises, how can women religious put up with this permanent inequality?

We get a hint of an answer from a paradoxical remark of Mary of the Incarnation, who had had experience of human and divine love: "Lord, I am quite happy to be nothing because, if I were not nothing, you would not be All." Here we see, with absolute clarity, the way a woman will revenge her own nothingness on God's immeasurable omnipotence. Since woman's capacity for domination is only equalled by her capacity for self-effacement, very few male mystics, with the exception of St Francis of Assisi, St John of the Cross and Charles de Foucauld, have been able to accept and carry on with a situation in which there was such a radical disproportion between their capacity for loving and the religious object of their love. Besides, women religious are too overwhelmed by the magnificence of their Beloved to be put off by their own lowliness. Their habitual acceptance of their position of adoring dependants reached a sublime conclusion in St Teresa of Lisieux's triumphant: "Since I've always done his will on earth, God will have to do mine in heaven!"

People usually say that chastity makes us "like the angels". This is true only in the sense that it makes us live "according to the spirit". But there is one point about a vow of virginity which could, as it were, make even the angels jealous: they have no bodies, and therefore cannot suffer; but we, with our bodies which are a prey to temptation and illness, can "make up what is wanting in the Passion of Christ". Mortification, therefore, which implies and, indeed, demands some degree of chastity, looks beyond mere control of one's senses. Within the context of the relativity inherent in all human activity—and under the supervision of obedience, without which one runs the risk of excess or deviation—chastity aims at an identification with Christ which supposes a generous participation in the moral suffering and physical pain with which the God-Man chose to redeem the world.

In some pathological cases, what one mystic called "the supplication made by a tortured body" can be motivated by a kind of disguised masochism. In our own day, some psychiatrists have urged prudence, the more strongly, in some cases, because their own contact with the world of consecrated religious has been almost entirely restricted to "cases": false vocations which have "gone off the rails" in a context in which, usually, innocence generates peace and joy compensates for devotion, or genuine vocations which have abruptly come to grips with interior demons who are part of an individual heredity, generated by overwork or, even, the spawn of the spirit of evil himself. Many of these difficulties deserve sympathetic and respectful handling. There have been many instances of co-operation between superiors or confessors and doctors who were men of deep faith and lively conscience.

There is no little comfort in the fact that well-guarded chastity can weather storms with the aid given it by an enlightened psychotherapy. On the other hand, it is sometimes surprising to see the credit certain religious circles give to the biased direction of psychiatrists who are believers, or unbelievers. The Holy Office recently handled the excesses sometimes committed in this field with a directive putting the clergy and religious on their guard about using psychoanalysis, and disapproving of the various "psychological" examinations and tests which candidates for some religious Orders and Congregations have been having to undergo in recent years.

In all of this, it is terribly important to remember that a nun is not a spinster: she is a spouse, and her vows constitute a nuptial commitment between her and God himself. Furthermore, recourse should be had to the divine Physician, who operates through the sacrament of penance and the Eucharist. Virginity is not frustration when it is self-surrender. A religious vocation is God looking at a creature and that creature returning God's glance with a devotion so rapturous that the joy should last until they both meet eternally. We can, at least, be absolutely sure of One of the couple.

Penance gives religious chastity a definite aspect of sacrifice, whether it is through work, stripping oneself of all superfluity, or keeping close check on one's licit impulses to friendship. Should it be forgotten, the Lord has a thousand ways of reminding us.

Chastity may be a long and hard struggle for someone who has always been chaste, whereas, on the other hand, a repentant sinner may find it not as difficult. St Mary Magdalen dei Pazzi only conquered herself after long and heroic mortification, while Charles de Foucauld said that, after his conversion, chastity was sweet and comforting. Easy or difficult, it must be accompanied by humility. And, once again, it is a grace which only one creature, the Virgin conceived without sin, received in all its fullness.

Except for the case (which is rarer than one might think) of a girl's being so physically attracted to marriage, enabling her to be a good wife, but not a true nun, there are the cases in which young women, who have unsuccessfully tried to acclimatize themselves to religious life, will not be any better suited to the married life. They cannot make a total self-surrender to God or to a man, and seem made for a single life whose value will lie in their work and whose joy will be in their friendships. Of Lazarus's two sisters, it was not Martha, with all her competence, who touched Christ's heart, but the impractical Mary, who was so moved by total love that she forgot all about eating, drinking and sleeping.

There must surely be many women religious whose vocation was awakened by a moving example of devotion which transcended the merely physical, and by a daily family life, which was built on mutual respect and self-sacrifice. It was on this example and experience that God built the vocation to a life which, in its own way, demands no less devotion and self-sacrifice.

Religious chastity is always understood to be perpetual, if not in its formulation, at least in its intention. Virginity is consecrated to God for ever, not merely for a few months or years, and a woman does not give herself to the divine Spouse for a short period of time but until death, just as another woman vows herself to a human husband for always. Sometimes a young woman whose entry into religious life has been delayed because of health or other reasons will, with her confessor's permission, make a private vow of virginity. In some instances, this consecration dates as far back as the girl's first Communion, or even before that time. There have been some privileged souls who, without any human influence being brought to bear on them, have consecrated themselves to God at the age of nine, or seven.

Chastity is so much an integral part of the religious life in general that even non-Christians do not consider the one without the other. When unbelievers bring pressure to bear to do away with the life of the vows, and of chastity in particular, it is because they more or less realize that one of the most moving and holy mysteries of religion is to be found in a voluntary and joyful sacrifice of earthly pleasures.

There are several religious Orders and Congregations which will not accept widows as candidates, though they may, in other instances, make exceptions in the case of illegitimacy, advanced age or lack of dowry. Their stand on this point is a question of principle and is not by any means an untenable deprecation of married life—St Paul himself consecrated widows to the service of the early Church—but rather the very understandable desire to offer to God individual souls who have never given themselves to anyone else.

God, who is the creator of purity, is also, of course, the restorer of purity. Virginity which has been lost through marriage or even through sin can be recovered in the "order of grace". All through the history of religious life in the Church, widows and converted sinners have been welcomed into convents. Widows have already experienced a life of self-forgetfulness, devotion and resignation during their married life, and all these are virtues admirably suited to religious life. Sinners, on the other hand, are living examples of the promise of Christ to Mary Magdalen: "Much shall be forgiven her because she has loved much."

One of the paradoxes of our age is that, all things being equal, a widow will bring to the religious life a greater spirit of detachment and a more highly developed adaptability, than a single woman of the same age, who has enjoyed independence and a career.

When John XXIII was speaking to a group of women religious of Rome and praised "the providential reserve of supernatural energies in the souls of these young women who consecrate to the service of the hierarchy the gifts which God has showered on woman", he was reaffirming one of the Church's most perennial and universally accepted attitudes: virginity which has been preserved from an early age for God's service is the ordinary preparation for the religious life. But perhaps the words "preserved . . . for God's service" need a little clarification: virginity may be preserved intact for the very highest motives but without any great impetus of charity. The religious vow of chastity, on the other hand, postulates a choice based on love. It is precisely in this distinction that we find the answer to a query frequently raised by psychiatrists: virginity which is not freely offered may have repercussions. Chastity motivated by the love of Christ, on the other hand, cannot, even if, especially in times as pagan as our own, the woman called by Christ has, through weakness or ignorance, known temptation, great struggle or sin.

The two other vows of religion are frequently less well understood than chastity. But while what is usually criticized about the vow of obedience is its rigour, the exact exercise of the vow of poverty is what is most often misunderstood.

Essentially, the vow of poverty prohibits the subject's disposal of anything without the superior's permission. A solemn vow of poverty means that the subject sacrifices even the *right* to property (and she must make her will during the sixty days immediately preceding profession), while a simple vow does not abolish the right to property, it forbids the *act* of ownership. A person with a simple vow of poverty may have personal possessions but cannot exercise ownership over them any more than if she did not have them.

In all this, it is, strictly speaking, a matter of material possessions. But when the vow of obedience is also in operation, even intellectual possessions, the talents, and their disposition and use, cannot be freely and independently exploited. As Fr Carpentier points out in his book,[1] the detachment postulated by a life of perfection extends to all created goods, whether they are considered as owned or merely on loan. Detachment like this, which applies to everything, eventually leads to the stripping of oneself. A subject does not use the community's possessions except in the sense that they are put at her disposal by Providence's delegates, her superiors. The individual who voluntarily takes on as radical a surrender as this does so because she wants to be as poor as the Holy Family were, and from a compassionate identification with Christ's poor.

The logical consequences of this situation, Fr Carpentier goes on, is that evangelical poverty must always seek simplicity in the manner of living, in accommodation, clothing and diet, and be ready to do without certain necessities, com-

[1] *Témoins de la cité de Dieu*, Paris, 1956 (English trans. *Life in the City of God*).

forts and "dignity of state". It must work itself out efficiently in the context of the economic conditions of its time and social environment.

As times change, of course, the exercise of religious poverty will change with them. For example, not many religious Orders today would have the necessary capital (or, perhaps, even the desire) to build a conventual church as large and magnificent as some of those scattered throughout Europe. On the other hand, these splendid old buildings are usually far colder and less comfortable than some less ambitious modern structures. It is, therefore, the spirit of poverty which is the important thing, and which makes a religious no less poor just because she is teaching in a centrally-heated classroom, or working in an attractively decorated hospital.

In the not too distant past, "charity" had something of a pejorative, and even sordid, connotation. Nuns in charge of orphanages and children's homes used to make their charges share their own view of poverty and dressed them in "sensible" and dull clothes. But it seems much more sensible that they now take some small advantage of the improvements they have instituted for the sake of those in their charge. Furthermore, the clearheadedness and reserves of energy which a nursing sister or a teacher needs mean that she should have adequate food and sleep. No one should be surprised, therefore, at reading or hearing that certain superiors have made these essentials available and even obligatory.

Nor is poverty outraged because a superior-general, who must travel great distances in a limited amount of time, travels by aeroplane rather than railway. And lay-sisters, who used to have to do work which would not even be expected of some servants, have greatly benefited by the sensible introduction of modern laundering and other housekeeping appliances.

On the other hand, a superior, mistress of novices, or even a teaching nun, may offend against her vow of poverty if she allows herself to be too attached to a certain residence, room, book or, even, position of responsibility. No one can emphasize too much the fact that poverty, while it is meant to help the individual to strip herself of self-love and possessions, must also be constructive: "emptying oneself" is only a means to an end, not the end itself. The social purpose of poverty is to set up opposition to the ordinary human desire to stand up for one's own rights and possessions, to prefer one's own goods to the common good. Anything a monk or nun makes should be well made, if only to exist as a living proof of the efficiency of a society based on fraternal love. Hence we have those magnificent abbatial churches which are worthy of the God whom they shelter, the splendid libraries of the mendicant Orders, or the model farms connected with and operated by various monasteries.

There is an analogy in what we have been saying about poverty to what we saw above about chastity: the individual does without possessions in order the better to say, "Yes", to divine love. But how is poverty regulated? By obedience, the vow which governs the other two. Obedience is renunciation, not only of things and other people, but of self.

If obedience means total dependence on another's will, how can people say that it leads to genuine liberty? Because it leaves God free to operate within the soul. Besides, doing what is pleasing to the heavenly Father, whose will is manifest through and by the rule as interpreted by superiors, is imitating Christ and following his example: "He became obedient, even to the death on the Cross."

What makes obedience so difficult nowadays in families, at work or to the law in general is that all think themselves more intelligent and capable than their superiors. In a religious community no one has any excuse for disregarding the Gospel which tells her to seek the last and lowest place. Thus, obedience which is prompt and entire, and leaves superiors complete freedom to decide what one will do and where, should stimulate a religious to fulfil her superior's wishes without paying any attention to her own apprehensions or, even, lack of enthusiasm. She must, besides, do all she can to bend even her judgement to accord with her superior's, who represents Christ, and to carry out the superior's will, recalling, if necessary, that, "though my superior has faults, God has none and it is he, after all, whom I serve".

A superior's authority is paternal and extends to the subject's personal life, within, of course, the limits of discretion which the Church imposes as necessary and which serve, in fact, as safeguards to this authority's foundation of love. A religious, consequently, lives always under obedience, even if she is far away from her superior and her community.

St Jane Frances de Chantal was aware that authority, in the hands of a certain type of woman, could be quite formidable. In most instances, of course, a woman's maternal instinct, transformed by grace, will temper her authoritativeness. Nevertheless, the Church has taken steps to ensure that a superior's authority never becomes tyranny. Since this tyranny may result from too long a term of office, or senility, the great majority of superiors are no longer elected for more than three, six or twelve years; after such a term, a prescribed interval must elapse before they may be re-elected. Benedictine abbesses, and some Cistercian abbesses, are almost the only superiors of women religious who are elected for life and are given a special liturgical blessing. On the other hand, the canonical visit of their local bishop, or his delegate, every five years gives him the opportunity to meet and speak with each of the nuns individually, and makes it possible for them to bring to his attention any abuse of authority or infraction of the rule which may have crept in.

The Code of Canon Law published in 1917 laid down the steps every candidate for the religious life must go through: six months as a postulant, one canonical year as a novice (which, in very many Congregations, is followed by a second year of novitiate), then annual vows, which are renewed three or five times, or vows for three or five years, followed by perpetual vows.

These perpetual vows may be either simple or solemn, the

latter, in the case of women religious, being made only by nuns living in major or minor papal enclosure.

When the young woman making her vows is *virgo intacta*, she may also be consecrated a virgin, according to a very old ceremony of the Church. The liturgical texts used during the ceremony have a sublime meaning which serves to underline the fact that, for time and eternity, the consecrated virgin belongs to the Lord.

Though the words used in the making of the simple vows may vary in length and content from one religious community to another, their burden is always and everywhere the same: a creature is making a voluntary and complete donation of herself to her Creator.

On this subject, it may be useful here to say a few words about the terms used in the Benedictine formula of profession, which is frequently misunderstood, or the cause of some confusion. A vow is made of "stability and conversion of life". This "conversion"—like the Poor Clare's "amendment of life" which often scandalizes the families and friends of daughters of St Clare, because it seems so unnecessary in their particular case—merely means that the individual binds herself to repentance for disorders in her past life. In this context, conversion means "a turning towards". A young woman turns herself towards life in a community, and undertakes to bend and adapt her attitudes and sentiments to the rule and her community's customs.

"Stability" here has two meanings: it is a vow of faithfulness to God, which implies poverty, chastity and obedience, and a vow to remain faithful to the Order, which excludes the possibility of changing from one Order to another.

Permission of the Holy See is necessary before a person may change from one Order or Congregation to another. It used to be the case that such permission was most easily granted when a member of a less strict Order wanted to join a stricter one; thus, for instance, a Benedictine nun who wished could, and can, ask permission to become a Cistercian.

Nowadays, good and sufficient reasons allow more numerous changes.

Some other Congregations, besides the Benedictines, add the vow of stability to the ordinary three "vows of religion", so that some nuns will promise not to change from their own, enclosed, Order to another, unenclosed (this is implicit in the commitment made by nuns under solemn vows), while others will bind themselves in a special way to the particular end of their Order, whether it be the service of the poor, the care of the sick or work for priests. Finally, some women religious, such as the Helpers of the Holy Souls, make a voluntary surrender of the merit they would ordinarily gain from their good works and apply those graces to the souls in purgatory; the Daughters of Wisdom, on the other hand, like true daughters of St Grignion de Montfort, surrender all their merit to the Blessed Virgin, for her to dispose of as she sees fit and necessary. Members of some Congregations of reparation make a private—the Church does not allow it to be public—vow to be "victims". All these individual approaches grow quite naturally out of the spirit and purpose of the particular Order or Congregation concerned.

Perpetual vows may not be made by anyone who is still a minor though, in the case of institutes of pontifical law, the pope may grant dispensations, while the local bishop has that right where an institute of diocesan jurisdiction is concerned.

Though an individual may leave her Congregation once her temporary vows have lapsed for any reason whatever, her community may not send her away except for serious spiritual reasons. They cannot dismiss her for reasons of health, for instance. The most that can be done is to suggest to a girl in temporary vows, whose health seems not likely to stand up to the rigours or demands of one institute's rule, that she seek admission into a community more adapted to her state of health.

No Congregation may receive a young woman who has been a postulant in another Congregation unless she presents dimissorial letters which state that she was free to leave the first group and did so honourably and without obligation on either part.

Exclaustration indults are granted for varying lengths of time to religious who must leave their cloister or live away from community life for reasons of health.

Though it rarely happens, nuns may sometimes be unfaithful to their vows and—except among the Cistercians, whose "Charter of Charity" makes pertinent provision—find it difficult to re-enter their community, though there do exist places where they may go and make retreats of rehabilitation.

Finally, common life obliges each member of a community to conform to the community's external order. Submission to rules and customs which have been adopted for the common good mean a visible incarnation of fraternal charity. On the other hand, however, it must not lead to disproportionate attachment to custom and usage, and the individual must always be ready to accept any change or modification approved by legitimate authority.

The supreme requisite of community life and fraternal charity is that each member puts aside all consideration of herself and her own needs, and finds supernatural joy in loving her sisters without restraint or stint. The particular mission of community life is to give an example of unity in a world torn by disunity and alienation, and to be an organization wherein all social problems are solved on the basis of fraternal love.

But to what extent can civil society imitate such an organization, seeing that it rests on a foundation which is, unfortunately, more material than those "cities of God" to which religious men and women give witness?

Civil society has its own greatest weakness in its relativity, while the religious life takes its strength and endurance from its attachment to the Absolute. Because it is a social order in which there should be no strikes, strife, disunity or disharmony, the religious life can be, to anyone who is unprejudiced, admirable and enviable. It is not a question of taking it or leaving it:

Christians in the world are forced to recognize it as a lesson in disinterestedness and many of them, if they are sincere in their admiration, are led to change their lives because of what they see. This is one reason why retreats made in monasteries and convents are so successful, and why young people whose schools are attached to or part of a religious house are so often permanently influenced for good by the example of selflessness and holiness they see all about them every day.

The religious life is unparalleled not only because it is a striving towards perfection, but because it is also a "state of the Church", where God alone is served. Religious communities live at the heart of the Church to point out the way to the celestial City to which, though their roads may be different, all Christians are journeying. The life of perfection of a religious, a life which is, as Fr Carpentier points out, "supernatural, mortifying, celestial, eucharistic and Marian", is the only way of life which obeys entirely the laws of the new world and life which were laid down in the Gospels. In a few words, then, the function of the religious life is to deify the world.

CHAPTER IV

THEIR PRAYER LIFE

The quality of a nun's prayer-life, no more than a lay person's, is not judged by the length of the spiritual exercises it involves though it may, of necessity, have more aspects and divisions to it. On the other hand, the maxim of St Francis de Sales, "Prayer: twenty-four hours a day", was no joke. The life of a nun, active or contemplative, should be one continuous prayer.

But if she is lost in God, how can she do her work? It is precisely because she is "lost" in God that her work and activity are effective. It is not, naturally, a question of allowing herself to wander off in a nihilistic evasion of reality and her obligations, even though she has pretensions to mysticism. What she does do is allow her will gradually and reasonably to be substituted for by the will of him who is love and intelligence itself. Prayer and obedience are the ordinary and most efficient means of achieving this substitution.

Usually, a nun will grow more and more suited to her vocation, and gradually become more effective in her apostolate, whether it is teaching, nursing, parish visiting or in the missions, as she fosters the realization of the Trinity dwelling within her, cultivates the great virtues and daily becomes more and more aware of the eternal truths.

There are several methods of uniting oneself to God in that silent colloquy with him which we ordinarily call prayer. God deals individually with each soul, and the substance of genuine prayer cannot be contained within easy recipes—nor is there one single way for all souls to become holy.

Though the supreme Teacher of prayer is the Holy Spirit, each great school of spirituality, and especially those founded by St Benedict, St Ignatius Loyola, St Teresa of Avila and St John of the Cross, St Francis de Sales, M. Olier and the Sulpicians, St John Baptist de La Salle and St Alphonsus Liguori, suggests a method aimed at purifying one's heart and recollecting one's soul, which are absolutely essential if grace is to come into the soul, whether there be sensible effects or not, and whether or not it leads to that "suspension of the powers" in what is called transforming union. In his *Methods of Mental Prayer*, Cardinal Lercaro suggests a practicable and objective synthesis of these various schools of spirituality.

One thing to be noticed about the prayer life is that it is just as possible for a lay-brother, who may be illiterate, to have a strong and deep prayer life as it is for a highly educated and scholarly priest. Though, strictly speaking, there are no longer illiterate religious, past centuries of the Church's history have seen some such religious attaining knowledge through their prayer which they would not have been able to acquire through the ordinary means. Scholars, on the other hand, may sometimes have to put aside their intellectual prowess and success (knowledge, after all, may lead to evil as well as to good), or at least realize their inadequacy before uncreated Wisdom.

One very important part of the prayer life of the Church's religious in general is the Divine Office. Women religious who have made solemn vows—who, technically, are the only ones who should be called "nuns"—are bound under pain of grave sin to recite it, or sing it, in Latin or the mother tongue. On the other hand, though the Divine Office is becoming more and more known and recited, even by lay-people, because of the active interest in things liturgical during the past few years, we should not overlook the fact that there are some women religious—45,000 Daughters of Charity and 14,000 Salesian Sisters, for example, and many missionaries—who are daily striving after perfection and do not sing or recite the Divine

Office nor even the Little Office of the Blessed Sacrament or of our Lady, which some contemplative Congregations use. Nor does it seem that their lives are any less holy or effective for that reason. There is a certain kind of "holy snobbery" which should be guarded against but which, under the cloak of a desire to do only the best and most recommended, ends up by imposing burdens which are scarcely suited to an individual community's members or its apostolate.

What many lay-people, even those with some familiarity with the religious life, forget or understand badly is that, without some longer or shorter daily period of prayer during which a religious is able to spend some time alone with God, the whole structure of the religious life would fall apart. Without the spiritual nourishment which, in the long run, is what really keeps him going, a busy apostle runs the risk of developing a taste for "terrestrial food", which may be temporarily satisfying but is not nourishing. In some isolated cases, of course, it almost seems that an individual religious is using his prayer life as an excuse for not performing his other duties. Also, one frequently hears people complain that the sisters in charge of such and such a hospital or clinic are never available because "they're always in the chapel". But, in this last instance at least, that time in chapel—and it is usually far shorter than the complaints would lead one to believe—is the only time the sisters have alone with Christ, who is, after all, their Bridegroom. And how many people would venture to criticize a lay woman who taught or was a nurse for hurrying home after a hard day's work to be alone with her husband and family, where she was sure of getting the affection and encouragement necessary to go on with her job from day to day?

CHAPTER V[1]

THE CONTEMPLATIVES

Out of the million or more women religious all over the world, about sixty thousand are members of contemplative Orders—which means that God has kept aside only six per cent. of this vast spiritual treasury for himself alone and to live lives of repayment and retribution for sinful mankind.

Because of an extraordinary privilege granted her by the Holy See, for some seven years the author has been visiting convents of major and minor papal enclosure in France and in other countries, when superiors and the local Ordinaries found such a visit convenient. Altogether, she has been in sixty or so convents, and has everywhere been struck by the evident happiness of the nuns and their singlemindedness in pursuing a life of withdrawal from the world and contemplation of the great supernatural truths.

There are from fifteen to eighteen hundred such contemplative convents scattered all over the world, and each of them has from ten to two hundred members who wear, according to the particular Order, a habit of white, black, brown, grey or blue or pink. Their life has changed less in recent times

[1] Information concerning the ordinary way of life, requirements for admission, etc., of the Congregations to be discussed in subsequent chapters, and of many other Congregations, can be found in the annual *Official Guide to Catholic Educational Institutions and Religious Communities in the United States* (Washington, D.C.) or the *Directory of Religious Orders, Congregations and Societies of Great Britain and Ireland* (Glasgow). Each of these books gives a brief but complete description of the various religious communities it lists, and also provides addresses where further necessary information may be obtained.

than have the religious dress, customs and apostolate of many active Congregations who must adapt themselves to the needs of changing times, obtain the professional qualifications required by the State and, in general, keep absolutely in touch with the demands of modern society in which they live.

At the same time, the older Orders have found it necessary, at times, to introduce modifications, if not changes, of their traditional rule because of their new candidates, who have been so affected by the wars and political instability of the world in which they have grown up, their tiring studies, or an unstable family life, the many legitimate exemptions they have been allowed from fasting and abstinence, and even the centrally-heated schools, homes and offices where they have spent so much of their early years. Diet and the matter of sleep have also been affected because many groups have found that regulations bearing on these points did not meet the demands caused in some cases by the sisters' having to take on some work, if only to make up for a curtailing of alms which, in the old days, constituted the convent's entire income. All these considerations, naturally, have also had a greater or less effect on the individual's penitential practices and austerities.

Some of the more austere Orders have established branch Congregations which women of delicate or less robust health may enter and enjoy the benefits of the mother-Order's spirituality and ascetical training.

One Congregation, the Oblates of Christ the High Priest, founded some twenty years ago at Madrid, have resisted all claims of modern needs to modify an austerity which some observers have found overwhelming. The Oblates firmly refuse to give in to nature except on the most necessary points and are constantly on the look-out for more and more difficult sacrifices in their life, which is dedicated to the sanctification of the priesthood.

Besides these matters, there have also been obvious changes in the ordinary prayers and spiritual exercises of many of the

Orders. Young people nowadays have, to some degree at least, been influenced by the great work which has been done in recent years in biblical and liturgical studies. They find that many vernacular prayers, written in the style and vocabulary of the seventeenth, eighteenth and nineteenth centuries, are no help whatever to their spirit of devotion and, in some instances, make no sense. One change along these lines has been the refocusing of the community's life, with the Mass as the centre and other community prayers drawn from or based upon the Divine Office and the liturgy. More opportunity for mental prayer has also been introduced in some places, an opportunity which the Carmelites have always enjoyed, since their foundress, St Teresa of Avila, considered that prayer is "an intimate commerce of friendship in which we often converse alone with God, by whom we know we are loved".

Many Catholic young people, raised in the social atmosphere of the various Catholic young people's movements, find the emphasis the Benedictines place on community life very attractive. "How good it is to live in the house of the Lord with one's brothers [or sisters]", and to join them in chanting the Divine Office and then, while working silently, to "ruminate over the Psalms", as St Bernard said. In this way, removed from contact with the world by grilles and cloister, a religious endlessly works at building a high and strong fortress of the Church's prayer. Because one must be part of the Church. There is no getting away from that.

When St Teresa of Avila said, "I am a daughter of the Church", how could she make this claim? And how are her spiritual daughters the Church's daughters? Because of their service of love lived out in a solitude bereft of every comfort, of even some legitimate liturgical embellishments, in which they seek only the "company of the sisters" within the limits laid down by mutual assistance and correction. "In the midst of the Church, my Mother, I shall be Love," wrote St Teresa of the Child Jesus and the Holy Face. Once a soul joins St John of the Cross in his desire for nothing, and has passed through the obscure night, the "self" is no longer an encumbrance, so much has it been absorbed into infinitely lovable Being. The change takes place quietly on a level deeper than the reason's discursiveness, and through a simple and non-resisting cooperation with the activity of the Holy Spirit. There would be a risk of some sort of "disincarnation" —which hovers over the experiences of yoga, Christian or not—if the soul's faculties were not directed at the sacred humanity of Christ and if there were not a constant filial recourse to Mary.

But humility is the best safeguard of confidence and balance in this situation. Carmelite asceticism does not aim at ecstasies, raptures or "private revelations", as so many people seem to believe. On the contrary, its purpose is simply to please God, who is loved to the extent that all creatures are forgotten. St Teresa of Lisieux's "I shall spend my heaven doing good upon earth" loses all its meaning unless it is understood as "I shall live on earth as though I were already in heaven". A Carmelite's apostolic mission is to love the world, but in the same way that a nuclear expert sets off an atomic device—from a distance.

There are forty thousand Discalced (that is, of the Teresan Reform) Carmelite nuns in every part of the world. They began establishing convents in non-Christian countries during the last century. Each of the convents is autonomous, but there has recently been a tendency to group themselves into federations.

In 1878, at the instance of Cardinal Manning and with the assistance of Fr Frederick Faber, the Carmel of the Most Holy Trinity was opened in London by nuns of the first French Carmel. There are now thirty-four Carmels in England, and thirteen in Ireland. St Teresa's reform was established in the United States in 1790, and there are now forty monasteries of Discalced Carmelites throughout the country.

An American Carmelite, Mother Catherine Thomas, has published a remarkable account of the life she and her sisters lead in their Carmel,[2] and great attention was drawn to the religious life by a documentary film made in a Carmel and televised by the B.B.C. a few years ago.

In a Carmelite monastery, the liturgy is less impressive and attractive than it is, say, in a Benedictine convent, though the spirit and effect of the liturgy is as apparent in a Carmelite as in a Benedictine. It has become almost proverbial to describe Carmelites as "vivacious and joyful", qualities to which, indeed, they have every right to lay claim, since every visitor to a Carmel leaves with a lasting impression of the great happiness and joy there.

Carmelites observe perpetual abstinence, have seven hours of uninterrupted sleep, and work alone and silently in their cells. Widows are accepted as candidates, and the constitutions do not fix any age-limit for admission. Converted sinners have always been admitted to Carmel. A Carmelite prioress is elected for a term of three years and may be re-elected for the same length of time.

Details of Carmelite life like these are quite well known, since there is no other body of contemplative nuns which has attracted so much attention and interest over the years. Furthermore, the life of a Carmelite was fully explained and shown for what it actually is by St Teresa of Lisieux's famous *Autobiography*. On the other hand, two less well-known Carmelites, whose works deserve greater attention and study, were Sister Elizabeth of the Trinity, of the Dijon Carmel, and the converted Jewess, Edith Stein, who, as Sister Theresia Benedicta a Cruce, was taken from her monastery at Echt, in Holland, by the Nazis and was executed in a concentration camp. The processes for beatification of both these nuns have been opened.

Calced Carmelites of the Ancient Observance have monasteries in Spain (where their Barcelona convent was deeply influenced by the teaching of the blind lay-brother, John of St Samson), Italy, Belgium and Germany. There are, besides,

[2] *My Beloved: the Story of a Carmelite Nun*, New York, 1955.

three Calced Carmelite monasteries in the United States, and one in England. Many smaller Congregations, of active or mixed life, have grown from the spirituality of St Teresa and St Teresa of Lisieux.

A group of nuns who are still more solitary than the Carmelites are the Carthusian nuns who, though they have not yet established any houses in English-speaking countries, deserve discussion here because of the age and importance of their Order.

A candidate to a Carthusian convent must be *virgo intacta*, and will not be admitted unless she is between twenty-one and twenty-eight. The life of Carthusian nuns is similar to that of Carthusian monks, though they are not as solitary as their brothers since the nuns do not each live in a separate little hermitage and all of them take their meals together in a refectory. Their prayer life is divided between the choir, where they chant the Mass and Office according to the old Carthusian liturgy, and their cells, where each of them recites privately the Office of the Blessed Virgin and, on some days, the Office of the Dead. Fast and abstinence are perpetual in a Carthusian convent, and the nuns may only receive visitors twice a year. Their solitude is relieved by five recreations in community each week, and they are allowed wide freedom to draw up their own schedule for work in their cells.

Benedictine life in England was demonstrated to great effect by the publication, a few years ago, of the biography of Dame Laurentia, Abbess of Stanbrook Abbey (Abbey of Our Lady of Consolation).[3] The Stanbrook community was first founded at Cambrai, Flanders, in 1625, by Dame Gertrude More, a descendant of St Thomas More; the nuns at Cambrai were, for many years, directed by the famous Dom Augustine Baker.

There are some twelve English Benedictine houses, attached to the English Congregation or independent, and some of them run schools and retreat houses. The Olivetan Benedictines, who wear a white religious habit, have two houses in England,

[3] *In a Great Tradition*, London, 1957.

each of which has founded a priory, one in Belgium and the other in Brazil.

The Benedictines of the Blessed Sacrament, who were founded by Mother Mechtilde of the Blessed Sacrament (Catherine de Bar) in 1653, have forty-six monasteries throughout the world, with one at Dumfries, Scotland.

In the United States, a Benedictine convent of the Primitive Observance was founded in Connecticut by a group of nuns from the Abbey of Jouarre. Altogether, however, there are some fifty Benedictine monasteries of pontifical or diocesan jurisdiction in the United States and, for the past 110 years, they have been realizing their Order's motto, *Ora et Labora,* in a combination of the contemplative life with the active. The nuns operate high schools, colleges and private academies, in addition to their regular religious duties.

In the light of all this evidence, it is clear that there is no real contradiction between the communal and eremitical choral and recitative, liturgical and individual tendencies in the religious life. The amount of each will vary, so that some contemplatives will even undertake work which seems more pertinent to an active or mixed life. Thus, there are convents of cloistered Benedictine, Passionist, Augustinian or Visitation nuns which have boarding schools in conjunction with their convents. In Ireland and Spain, Poor Clares, whose vow of enclosure has been mitigated to some extent, teach and instruct poor children. On the other hand, any work which will mean that they come into regular or frequent contact with externs is forbidden to Cistercian, Carthusian, Carmelite, Servite and Redemptorist nuns.

Something of a key to the Cistercian life is in the short sentence: "There is no recreation". Except when it is broken by the Mass and the Divine Office, silence is perpetual (except, also of course, in case of necessity) in a Cistercian house, and it generates the pure, complete and human joy which Fr Louis Bouyer has suggested is the keynote of Bernardine spirituality. A candidate for the Cistercian nuns must have strong health and perfect emotional and psychological balance if she is to persevere until death—and most Cistercian monks and nuns live to a very old age. During her life as a Cistercian, a nun will never use her voice except in choir, where the chant is somewhat more sombre than in other Benedictine monasteries, and she will have much manual and hard work to do. After spending several hours each day standing in choir, and several more at hard work, a Cistercian nun goes to bed in a dormitory, where she sleeps on a thin mattress laid on boards. She is never, therefore, what most of us would call comfortable.

Nor is she ever alone, since the Cistercian existence is based strongly on community life and, should she, for instance, receive the grace of performing miracles, she cannot be tempted to pride and feel she will one day be canonized: she has willingly undertaken complete and perpetual anonymity.

"The way of life of the Order of Poor Ladies which the Blessed Francis has instituted is this: to observe the Gospel of our Lord Jesus Christ while living in obedience, without personal property of any kind, and in chastity." This is the beginning of the Rule which was adopted by St Clare and the first Franciscan nuns in the thirteenth century and which is now lived in 649 monasteries all over the world. Some of the Poor Clares, the Urbanists, follow a rule which was mitigated for them by Pope Urban IV, and others, who are called Colettine Poor Clares, living according to the Rule as it was reformed by St Colette of Corbie in the fifteenth century. There are other small groups of these nuns who follow various mitigated or reformed versions of their rule.

St Francis of Assisi's ideal of close and constant imitation of the poor and humiliated Christ demands a complete and joyful renunciation of goods of any kind. The Poor Clares, except in a few instances, live completely on the alms given them. They rise for the night Office, observe perpetual abstinence and, in most of their convents, are barefoot. Changes in this regime may be made at the discretion of the abbess, who is elected for three years and may be re-elected for a similar term, providing that current canon law does not legislate against such a re-election. Life in their convents is, not surprisingly, of the greatest simplicity which generates an intense family spirit.

Many cloistered and contemplative communities have grown up from the Franciscan Third Order. The Annonciades (Order of Our Lady) were founded in 1501 by St Joan of France, the repudiated wife of King Louis XI of France. They have their own rule, which is definitely Franciscan in spirit, since it was drawn up by a Franciscan friar, Fr Gabriel Mary, for the ex-queen, who was a Franciscan tertiary. They recite the Divine Office in choir, are strictly enclosed, and keep abstinence four times a week and always at the evening meal. Their own Third Order, the Order of Peace, is unique in that it does not impose upon its members any fasting, alms-giving, or wearing of a scapular or medal; instead, members are bound to do everything they can to promote peace among their neighbours and to banish every remnant of hate from their thoughts, words and deeds.

Dominican religious follow what is basically the Rule of St Augustine modified by their own particular constitutions. They live an austere life—night Office, perpetual abstinence, chapter of faults, during which they accuse themselves and one another of infractions against the Rule—but it is a life of great liberty, sustained by and built upon choral recitation of the Office.

The Dominican love of study which made many medieval convents—such as the one at Unterlinden in Alsace, for instance—famous in history has lasted down through the centuries. In many cases, these intellectual pursuits have to be curtailed in order that more mundane occupations may be followed, occupations which, unlike study and scholarship, pay for the upkeep of the house and leave the nuns free for the "luxury" of contemplation.

Some convents of Dominican nuns have recently begun to

accept women of poor or uncertain health as candidates. Others have developed their own "speciality" within the great Dominican family, and centre their religious life round adoration of the Blessed Sacrament or perpetual recitation of the Rosary. One congregation of Dominican sisters, the Dominican Sisters of Bethany, were founded with the idea of giving women who, for whatever reason, have spent some time in prison the opportunity of entering the religious life. This group has recently been established in the United States.

The Order of the Visitation, which was founded by St Francis de Sales to make the contemplative life more accessible to widows and other women who could not support the austerities of the older Orders, is also based on St Augustine's rule. Though the life of the Visitation nuns is somewhat easier and less strict—but by no means "softer"—than the Carmelites', for instance, there are still some details of their life which, it seems, might be changed or adapted to modern life. Thus, today's young women invariably find the Divine Office and plainchant more attractive than the Little Office of the Blessed Virgin, which Visitation nuns sing on three notes only. On the other hand, it is difficult to believe that a Visitation nun, even the most modern, would want to surrender the grille which protects the intimacy of her prayer life, the daily occupation which motivates all her other activities.

Though there are no physical austerities habitually connected with a Visitation nun's life, she must nevertheless live in the most detailed obedience and in a detachment which extends to everything. The many small regulations covering even the most apparently insignificant activity are destined, according to St Jane Frances de Chantal (St Francis de Sales' collaborator in the foundation of the Visitation), to form "strong and courageous daughters whose daily life and work flow from a solid and dynamic holiness". Community life and relations within a Visitation convent are so thoroughly imbued with charity that even women who enter late in life, after having managed their own homes perhaps, have little or no difficulty in adapting themselves to even the smallest detail of the life. This is a life in which restraint and self-discipline lead to great love.

Also part of the Augustine family are the several groups of Canonesses Regular—of the Lateran, of Perpetual Adoration, of the Holy Sepulchre. The Canonesses Regular of the Mercy of Jesus are nursing sisters and, with the Ursulines, they were the first women religious in Canada.

The Congregation of Notre Dame, which was founded by St Peter Fourier and Blessed Alix Le Clerc, are a teaching group and they, like the Canonesses of the Mercy of Jesus, observe only minor enclosure. The Celestial Annonciades, however, who were founded at Genoa in 1604 by Victoria Fornari-Strata "to thank God for the grace of the Incarnation and to pray that the Good News of the divine Mysteries be brought to the farthest parts of the world", bind themselves to their cloister by a fourth vow. Their only visitors are their close relatives, to whom they speak through a board pierced with small holes which is set up behind the ordinary grille of the parlour; their parents are the only people who may actually see them.

In England, the Bridgettine nuns—the Order of the Most Holy Saviour—possess a strictly contemplative monastery in Devon at Syon Abbey, a direct descendant with unbroken continuity of the pre-reformation house of that name. There are also Brigittine Sisters. The original Rule of St Bridget, followed by the nuns of Syon Abbey, was adapted to the needs of modern times by Mother Elizabeth Hesselblad for the use of the sisters founded by her.

Passionist nuns, founded by St Paul of the Cross, lead a life of great austerity and mortification: they rise for the night Office, which is always recited and not chanted, except during Holy Week; they are barefoot; they observe long periods of fast and abstinence. Their monastery at Lucca, Italy, is the centre of devotion to St Gemma Galgani, a stigmatic of the late nineteenth century who, because of ill-health, could only be a Passionist by desire.

Redemptorist nuns, who were urged by their founder, St Alphonsus Liguori, "to learn from God alone the art of loving him", accept candidates with weak health for their life, which is between that of the Carmelites and of the Visitation.

Living a life vowed to the four ends of sacrifice—adoration, contrition, thanksgiving and petition—the Servants of the Most Blessed Sacrament, whose institute was founded by St Peter Julian Eymard, make adoration of the Holy Eucharist the "object of their affections, source of their happiness, and end and object of all their activity". Each sister spends an hour of adoration before the Blessed Sacrament every twenty-four hours. Convinced, however, that their apostolate should not be restricted to the already existing convents of their community in France, Belgium, Italy, Canada, Brazil, Australia and the United States, they have recently established a community in Africa. Theirs is a community of pontifical jurisdiction and, like many other congregations, they have abolished the category of lay-sister.

Among the many groups of religious women which are based on Ignatian spirituality is the Congregation of Marie Reparatrice. Founded by Baroness d'Hooghvorst with the double purpose of eucharistic adoration and of "taking the place of Mary", the congregation now has sixty-two convents distributed through thirteen provinces. Also Ignatian are the Daughters of the Heart of Jesus and the Religious of Our Lady of the Retreat in the Cenacle, who conduct retreat houses for women and members of the clergy. Both these groups are enclosed.

Spanish contemplatives include the Minims, who were founded by St Francis of Paula and bound by him to perpetual lenten fast and abstinence: no meat, milk, butter or cheese; the Hieronymites, who are direct descendants of the spiritual family founded by St Jerome and St Paula; the Conceptionists, who were founded by Beatrice da Silva and are white-habited Franciscans; the Trinitarians, Mercedarians and Mantellate Servites.

The Sisters of the Holy Ghost, who are under the direction of the Divine Word Fathers, have within their congregation a group of enclosed contemplative religious whose life is vowed to adoration of the Blessed Sacrament. Because of their distinctive habit, these sisters are frequently called the "Pink Sisters".

There are, in France or of French origin, two contemplative Congregations which are, however, not enclosed. First, the Oblates of the Eucharist, whose lives are spent working and praying for more priestly vocations and the sanctification of the clergy, work among the chronically ill, keeping themselves, in spirit at least, always before the Blessed Sacrament. The second group, who are still less enclosed because their particular apostolate is to be the "leaven" in infidel countries, are the Little Sisters of the Sacred Heart who, like the Little Sisters of Jesus, are spiritual daughters of Fr Charles de Foucauld. They adapt their life and daily programme to the customs, diet, and the rest of the country in which they are living in the hope of gaining candidates for their fraternities—as their convents are called—from among the native population. Their double function as contemplatives and missionaries is explained by this saying of Father de Foucauld: "The more we ask God our Spouse for the grace to love him with all our heart, forgetful of everything which is not he, the more we shall be able to do good for all mankind".

Very similar to this vocation, though, of course, different in their own ways because of the differences of place and culture, is the life led by the Missionary Recluses of Jesus and Mary, in Canada, and the Sisters of Galilee, who are contemplative religious of the Melkite rite; they were trained by the Poor Clares of Nazareth.

Thus we see, after reviewing this whole variety of the many contemplative Congregations and Orders, that even the apostolate of a contemplative is coloured and affected by the ends and aims of her Congregation, and by the direction in which that Congregation's inspiring spirituality leads her. The lives of contemplative nuns in their many varieties are a further proof of the vitality of the Church in the twentieth century.

CHAPTER VI

MISSIONARIES

"It is now about eight hundred years since women played any public rôle in the Church. And to anyone who wonders that women's rôle in Church affairs should deserve any comment at all, we can only say that God chooses his own instruments." This is what St Vincent de Paul said about the time that he was busy organizing the first group of Daughters of Charity. We ought not to forget that it has been through the breach opened up by the sisters in the famous white cornets that so many thousands of generous young women have been able to step into a wide variety of apostolic labours. And it was only because they could not avail themselves of the opportunity to join in the work of the Vincentian Fathers in Madagascar that the Daughters of Charity were not the first of the Church's women missionaries *in partibus infidelium*. Wars had stirred up disease and epidemics in France and, "leaving God to serve God", they applied themselves the more assiduously to work at home, all the while building up those reserves and traditions of self-sacrifice and courage which would eventually bring them to the battlefields of the Crimea and culminate in some of their number being the first women religious to be martyred in China, in 1870.

As a matter of fact, the first women religious who became missionaries were members of institutes which had not been founded as missionary groups. In 1638, Augustinian Canonesses of the Mercy of Jesus left for Canada with

Ursulines from Tours, among whom were Mme de la Peltrie and the venerable Marie of the Incarnation; they were followed by Marguerite Bourgeoys, who was to found the Congregation of Notre Dame at Montreal, and Jeanne Mance, the foundress of the Hôtel-Dieu of Montreal and a laywoman whose life of dedication can serve as an example to young women in these days when we see so many new states of perfection growing up within the Church.

New France has been one of the world's most civilized countries for so long a time that we are apt to forget the great hardships and danger these pioneers had to face. Despite these difficulties, religious life in Canada has flourished from the very beginning and today, in addition to the sixty European religious congregations which now have establishments in the country, there are fifty-five congregations which are essentially Canadian.

Thinking back on what these first women missionaries had to go through, we cannot help admiring them for their endurance and courage, to say nothing of their patience, which must have been sorely tried by their having to lead a life of the utmost hardship while remaining faithful to a rule which was inflexible and inadaptable. They were pioneers; they had to do everything for the first time and had no one else's experience to counsel or direct them.

We are also sometimes too apt to forget that the early development of Canada—and of the entire New World, in fact—owed a great deal to the decisive and effective rôle played by women religious. They channelled their great spiritual reserves towards providing education, hospital care and welfare services to the early pioneers and thereby preached the Gospel, not in words, but by self-sacrificing activity.

Since the seventeenth century, Sisters of St Paul of Chartres have been working in Guiana. Later, the Sisters of Christian Instruction began their apostolate in China, and the "Blue Nuns", the Sisters of the Immaculate Conception of Castres, set out for the mission fields in Senegal and Gaboon. Other missionary groups were the Sisters of St Joseph of Cluny, founded by Blessed Anne-Marie Javouhey (whom Louis-Philippe called "a great man"), and the Sisters of St Joseph of the Apparition, who were founded by St Emily de Vialar. Members of this latter Congregation went to the missions in Algeria and shortly thereafter abolished the category of lay-sisters because the Algerians, seeing the lay-sisters' silver rings (choir nuns' rings were gold), thought they were being punished or humiliated by not being allowed gold rings.

In 1876, a group of members of the Society of Marie Reparatrice broke away from their mother society and, under the leadership of Mother Mary of the Passion, organized themselves into the Franciscan Missionaries of Mary.

Many of these missionary sisters were recruited by priests and bishops who had returned to their home countries to rest or to seek support for their work. Many others, on the other hand, were members of Congregations founded by missionary Congregations of men, to help in the work of preaching the Gospel to all nations. The sisters were organized to operate schools, dispensaries, leprosaria and generally to dispense the more material aspects of Christian charity. Thus, the Missionary Sisters of Our Lady of the Apostles were founded by Fr Augustin Planque, co-founder of the Society of the African Missions of Lyons; Cardinal Lavigerie, who founded the White Fathers, organized the Sisters of Our Lady of Africa in 1869 to carry on the apostolate among Moslem women of Northen Africa; other female Congregations were initiated by the Society of Mary, the Paris Society for the Foreign Missions, the Holy Ghost Fathers and other such groups. At the same time, of course, there were formed Congregations of women religious which were independent of any already existing men's Congregations and were completely missionary in their end and aims.

How were the training and attitudes of these missionary Congregations different from those of others, many of which were several hundred years older than the new groups? First of all, of course, the candidate for a missionary Congregation sought acceptance by the group fully aware that, once she had taken her vows, she might be sent off to a foreign mission and never, perhaps, see her homeland and family again. (In Congregations which are not primarily missionary, superiors do not send a nun to the mission fields unless she has asked to be sent or otherwise shown that she would be able to carry out such an assignment with joyful obedience.) Also, in order to be an efficient apostle of Christ in Africa or Asia, the missionary nun has to have a thorough knowledge of the life, customs and problems of the people among whom she will be working. She must also be able to stand up to the rigours of tropical or Arctic climates, have a reasonable facility for learning the native language and be adaptable to ways of thought and attitudes quite foreign, perhaps, to her own. Though it is no longer very likely that her labours will be rewarded with martyrdom, the missionary nun today has the consolation of knowing that she will be able, in case of necessity, to baptize any child or catechumen among her mission people.

Once the door had been opened for women in the missions, other Congregations took up the task of educating the children of leading pagan families in those areas. Thus, the Helpers of the Holy Souls opened schools in China, and the Ursulines began to work in Java, Alaska and the Transvaal. As they introduced their students to the learning of the West, these nuns did not imagine that they would be able to effect mass conversions; on the contrary, the message of Christ and his Church was learned almost unnoticed by the daughters of brahmins, mandarins and emirs, though it may not have borne fruit immediately, or even for generations.

Contemplatives, too, soon began to give apostolic witness in the missions. The Poor Clares went to the Holy Land, the Visitation nuns to Syria, Cistercians to Japan, and Carmelites to Lebanon and the Far East. It may be that some orientals, whose religious traditions have made them withdrawn and introspective, have discovered the aspects of Christianity which are more sympathetic to them in these contemplative convents than in more active groups. Buddhist and Hindu nuns soon changed their garb and ritual to join in adoring "in spirit and in truth" uncreated Love.

Very shortly, Congregations of native women were founded or encouraged by the various European missionary groups. On this point, it may be worth while to remark, in passing, how unfortunate it was in the beginning that so many native religious Congregations were hampered in their natural growth and development by being forced to adopt European dress, ways of thinking and, in some instances, physical attitudes in prayer. The situation was all the more ironic considering that it was, after all, in the East that the West first saw the Star shining.

Now that we are seeing an end to "colonialism", however, and since so many former mission countries are being given their own bishops and clergy, what remains for European missionary Congregations to do? Are they to return to Europe and take up teaching posts or hospital work?

The fact that so many mission fields have benefited by the scientific and technical progress of Europe and the New World does not mean that their problems are once and for all solved. Schools will still be necessary, hospitals continue to need staffs and supervisors, orphans still need love and care. And if there is a desperate lack of vocations in Europe, the United States and Canada, which have been Christian areas for many centuries now, how great must the lack of workers be in other, more recently Christian places?

Besides these foreign mission fields, there are also the missions at home. Modern society has grown rapidly during the past two centuries, and has made gigantic strides in progress and accomplishment. Almost in step with those advances, however, has been a gradual secularization and de-Christianization. Whereas in an African mission area, for example, a Christian would say that his family has been

Christian for only two or three generations, there are too many places in Europe and the New World where people would say that, *until* two or three generations ago, their family had been Christian. Obviously, the Church needs workers who will specialize in this work and dedicate themselves to bringing their own countrymen and society back to God.

In the United States, this problem was complicated by the need to help millions of immigrants remain faithful in a country whose language and religious customs were strange to them. The Missionary Sisters of the Sacred Heart, founded in Italy in 1880 by St Frances Xavier Cabrini, carries out vast apostolate among Italian immigrants to the United States, and there are many other Congregations whose work is principally among the various other national immigrant groups.

CHAPTER VII

THE ACTIVE LIFE

How do religious Congregations arise?

"They come from nothing," I was told by a man once, "from nothing, because they are works of God and it is he alone who directs and protects them with infinite wisdom and goodness."

Like the other works of God, religious Congregations are many and varied—a fact overlooked by those who claim that there are too many of them, and that they are too varied and should be reorganized into a few, "basic" groups.

And would a Franciscan sister want to be a Dominican? Would a member of a Congregation which is Ignatian or Vincentian in spirit agree to becoming Benedictine? It should be remembered that a woman religious is what she is, and thinks as she does, not because her community has such and such an apostolate, but because she has been trained in and formed by the particular spirituality of her Congregation. Besides, not everyone can do everything, and there is a strong element of practicality in having the various religious families share among themselves the many different tasks the Church has to do. Finally, such things as national attitudes and racial mentalities influence the particular spirit and energy of one or another Congregation.

In the United States, there are seventy Congregations which were formed and have developed there, alongside branches of the more than sixty Congregations whose members first went to America from France, the thirty from Italy, twenty each from Germany and Canada, twelve or so from England, Ireland and Spain, and the others in smaller numbers originally from Austria, Holland, Portugal, Switzerland, Latin America, Poland, Lithuania, Hungary and Ukrainia. Some of them went to the New World as missionaries, others were refugees; in each case, Providence used its own means to provide the necessary spiritual aids for the new and growing country.

Apostolic necessities in the modern world have conspired to increase, if not in numbers, at least in respect of their activities, many previously small, local Congregations. And at a time when some active Congregations, whose spirit and activities are similar, have decided to join forces and mutually sacrifice cherished but non-essential customs, and when several previously autonomous monasteries of the same Order agree to confederate under a single superior general, establish a general novitiate, revise their particular constitutions to make them more universally applicable, and generally co-operate in making the work of the entire organization more unified and widespread (by taking on missionary work or education, for instance), it was reassuring to hear John XXIII encouraging thus the new religious Congregations being formed to meet modern apostolic needs:

> The Church is always ready to give audience to the voice of those groups who, like their predecessors in past ages, beg permission to form themselves into holy and approved associations, and are waiting for encouragement to take on the tasks created by the needs of our times. After examining them carefully and allowing experience to prove them—as is her way in matters of such importance and responsibility—the Church incorporates into the Mystical Body these organizations whose variety and multiplicity make one think of the variety and beauty of flowers (Discourse to the Religious of Rome, January 29th, 1960).

People who oversimplify and would like to see religious Congregations reorganized should think about these words of

Pope John, remembering that we live in an age when there is a tendency to stultify and paralyse the dynamism of eternal values. As far as the "Great Adventure" of the religious life has been pursued, we are still a long way from the end of its possibilities.

The Vocation Guidance Council of the Archdiocese of New York publishes a brochure called *These Sisters serve New York*, which lists and briefly describes the Congregations of women working and praying in one of the world's largest urban centres. All of them are not "native" American groups; the Sisters of the Blessed Sacrament, who "strive through their essentially eucharistic vocation to make the millions of Indians and coloured people one with them in Christ", were founded by Mother Katherine Drexel in Philadelphia; the Sisters of Our Lady of Christian Doctrine were founded in New York by Mother Marianne of Jesus (Marion Gurney); and the Sisters of Divine Compassion were founded by Mother Maria Veronica (Caroline Starr) in New York—but they all work side by side with the Daughters of Divine Charity, a group begun in Vienna by Franziska Lechner, and with the Missionary Sisters of the Sacred Heart, Mother Cabrini's daughters.

Another United States Congregation are the Corpus Christi Carmelites, whose spirit, of course, has strong ties with the Spain of St Teresa of Avila, and who have particular devotion to the French Carmelite, St Teresa of Lisieux. The Sisters of St Dorothy and the Daughters of St Paul are both of Roman origin.

Before being spiritual daughters of Mother Elizabeth Seton, the Sisters of Charity of New York and the Sisters of Charity of St Elizabeth were spiritual "grand-daughters" of St Vincent de Paul, whose French genius made practical application of the Middle-Eastern Paul of Tarsus' "The charity of Christ urges us . . ."

Conversely, the Sisters of SS. Cyril and Methodius, who were founded in Scranton, Pennsylvania, in 1909 "to instruct the children of the Slovak immigrants who came in great numbers to America at the beginning of the century", might not have been able to establish themselves securely if a Sister Servant of the Immaculate Heart of Mary, whose Congregation is native American, had not agreed to allow candidates for the new community to make their early training among her community's novices. The Sisters of SS. Cyril and Methodius are a flourishing Congregation now and more than fulfil the promise made to every candidate: "Every capability finds expression in the service of God."

An American missionary group are the Foreign Mission Sisters of St Dominic—who are better known as the Maryknoll Sisters, and with the priests and lay-brothers of Maryknoll are part of one large family of devoted and zealous missionaries. Besides the members of their cloistered branch, which was founded in 1932, the Maryknoll Sisters have had members at work in China, Korea, Manchuria, Japan, Ceylon, Peru, Bolivia, Chile and the Marshall Islands. They are

> engaged in all types of mission work at home and abroad. Hence there are many diversified occupations available to young adventurers of the Lord. Among the sisters there are doctors, nurses and medical technicians of all kinds; teachers on all scholastic levels; domestic workers, social service workers, office workers, catechists trained to teach religion, writers, editors, photographers and artists. All are needed to bring home to America the needs of the missions.

Whether she is working among the *birrichini* of Turin, the *poulbots* of Montmartre or on New York's Lower East Side, a Salesian Sister—a Daughter of Our Lady, Help of Christians—will bring to her apostolate that combination of practical confidence in Providence and deep prayer which so characterized St John Bosco, her Congregation's founder.

There is a salutary vigour generated by this healthy national feeling among some religious Orders, which makes them adapt themselves, first of all, to the difficulties and needs nearest at hand. Conversely, other religious groups, such as the Little Sisters of Jesus, of Fr Charles de Foucauld, aim at rising above any and all national differences and divisions. In one of their publications, the Little Sisters say: "If considered necessary, after perpetual vows, a Little Sister may even change her nationality to that of those to whom she is consecrated."

It remains true, of course, that a woman religious may, as a woman, cherish her nationality as much as she does, as a religious, her Congregation's habit. Patriotism, after all, is a virtue connected with the practice of the fourth commandment. Besides, in the long run, once a soul has enlisted in that army of the peace of the Gospels, it no longer has any enemy except the Devil.

Just as recent as this readiness to change nationality for apostolic reasons, but even less open to discussion because it is, *prima facie*, so clearly an efficacious instrument of zeal, is some Congregations' decision to adopt, wherever necessary, "the liturgy, discipline and jurisdiction of the Oriental rites". Some sisters, after making this change over to the "more primitive and original" disciplines of the Church, have found that their return to the sources, as it were, of Christian spirituality has kindled their devotion and stimulated their spiritual life to a degree far outweighing the almost inevitable feelings of strangeness connected with such a change.

Why should Rose Hawthorne Lathrop, daughter of Nathaniel Hawthorne, have renounced her life of luxury and moved into a three-room flat on New York's Lower East Side to begin her Servants of Relief for Incurable Cancer? Because God called her to look after his suffering in a way to which her generosity could not help but respond. But suppose science should one day find a cure for cancer; what will become of her Congregation then? There will be others of God's sufferers to whom to dedicate their lives.

The Daughters of the Heart of Mary imitate the hidden life of Mary in an institute which was founded in France by Fr de la Clorivière, a member of the then suppressed Society of

Jesus, during the Revolution. Members of the Congregation do not wear any distinctive habit, are not called by a "name in religion" and may, if it is necessary, remain living with their families. They have modern imitators in the Sisters of Our Lady of Providence, who work in Rhode Island, and the Missionary Oblates of the Immaculate Conception, a Congregation working in Massachusetts. Both these groups wear plain street-length dresses and ordinary hats, as their habits.

Another U.S. Congregation, who say that they are "the modern American religious Congregation of home missioners", are the Sisters of the Divine Spirit, who live according to "a modified rule: taking yearly vows, doing evening catechetical and social work, taking a yearly vacation of at least one week, driving a car, and visiting and helping one's parents in case of illness".

Some founders and foundresses needed great reserves of courage and determination to overcome prejudices and habits making it impossible for women religious to undertake certain types of work. Mother Anna Dengel, for example, was impressed by the need for trained women doctors and medical technicians to work among the Moslem women of India and organized the Society of Catholic Medical Missionaries. From the Society's motherhouse in Philadelphia, sisters trained as doctors, nurses, pharmacists, dieticians and medical technicians go out to mission fields all over the world.

This short review of the ramifications of apostolic work which prompted the foundation of so many and varied active Congregations shows how Providence has always been able to make use of any sort of human activity, even national catastrophe, to raise up the workers most needed in its vineyards. Opportunity has always been found to make use of essentially feminine characteristics to meet needs and demands felt in the Church.

A sister's consecrated instinct towards charity has inevitably been drawn to the most miserable and abandoned, to people most in need of help and encouragement. It is legendary among many Congregations of women that, when a superior general sends out a call for workers in a mission leprosarium, for example, she always receives ten times as many volunteers as she needs. Many of these Congregations have been immeasurably aided by their lay-sisters, who sacrifice any ambitions to a missioner's life in order to remain at home and do the ordinary tasks—tasks and services without which no well-organized group could survive. It is their task to see that their missionary sisters are well fed, comfortably clothed, and have neat and tidy homes to return to after a long day's work.

The Church has always depended upon women to work for her as servants—and it is not difficult, when visiting a rural church, to tell whether the parish is fortunate enough to have a parochial assistant to keep the church clean, arrange fresh flowers for the altar, and otherwise take care of the church's "housekeeping".

At the same time, it used to be the case that, apart from the corporal works of mercy, a woman religious's work was very limited. A girl who had been lucky enough to have received a good education, would probably, in most Congregations, have found there was little or no opportunity to use what she had learned. One striking exception to this state of affairs were the Helpers of the Holy Souls who, because of their solid Ignatian formation, from the very beginning were active and convincing apologetists in Europe and Asia, particularly among the higher classes. On the other hand, some missionary groups have been taken aback by the extent of religious knowledge and interest they have encountered among the poor and lower classes, and some Sisters of Charity of St Paul of Chartres have expressed their gratitude for the theological training they were given, training which stood them in good stead in some areas where Marxism had already started to gain a foothold.

Members of active religious Congregations are beginning to work in fields which, at first glance, are not as directly apostolic as, for instance, is teaching. Music, painting, sculpture and literature are some of the areas in which they are beginning to work—and be noticed. Not long ago, for example, a Handmaid of the Sacred Heart, whose Congregation was founded in Madrid in 1877 by Blessed Mary of the Sacred Heart (Rafaëla Poras), had a "one-man show" in a Madrid gallery which was greeted with very high praise from critics. Another member of the same institute gave a series of apologetic lectures on the television in Ecuador, which resulted in the television station's being awarded for transmitting the best Catholic programme of the year.

Thus, though a woman religious's basic attitude must be that she is always ready to do whatever she is told, more and more superiors are taking advantage of each individual's particular talents and aptitudes. On the whole, of course, this development should not be surprising since not everyone is capable of doing every job, and most people work more efficiently at a task for which they are suited and, if possible, equipped. Thus, the years of training necessary before a sister can go into the apostolate pose more problems than merely financial ones to superiors. Some courses of training require reserves of concentration, endurance and physical stamina if they are to be concluded successfully. In many instances, therefore, a candidate for a particular Congregation or Order may have to ask: "Is the rule of the Congregation adapted to girls who are not very strong?" And in many cases the answer will have to be: "The rule is, yes—but our work is not."

On this point, the Ursulines have had this to say: "A teaching nun's life demands lengthy studies and lifelong work —and the time actually spent in teaching is only a small part of this labour."

Well, then, how is a young woman to choose the one Congregation, among so many, which is best suited to her talents and capabilities—and in which she will be most useful and happy? In most instances, fortunately, she has the example of the nuns teaching her at school to attract her to or dissuade her from one Congregation. Perhaps the recollection, the goodness and obvious happiness of one of her teachers will make her decide that she, too, should become a member of that group. Or perhaps she will pick up and read a book about a Congregation or one of its members which will help her decide. Something else which is helping many young women nowadays to select their future religious family is the frequency of programmes on radio and television documentaries in which listeners and viewers are given a good idea of the life, sights and sounds within one convent or another.

However she comes to her final decision, a young novice enters a life in which she will be, once for always if she perseveres, the spouse of Christ. Far from being static and stultified, her religious life will mean years and years of charity adapting itself to her neighbour's needs gracefully and kindly. It means self-sacrifice which does not diminish when habit of virtue makes it less painful, but which increases as charity makes her ever more aware of others' needs. This fact has been the underlying explanation for the adaptations and modifications in recent years in many active Congregations' rules. In certain instances, some groups felt that they would be lacking in virtue to allow themselves any change at all, even if their work demanded some variation, and it needed the advice of bishops and even of the Sacred Congregation for Religious before they could accept the changes involved with an easy conscience. It is to their credit, of course, that in these situations they did not anticipate the approbation of the Church and, once the change had been suggested as advisable, they deferred to the Church's wisdom.

CHAPTER VIII

THE SISTERS OF CHARITY

"You are not religious, but lay people," their founder used to insist to them. But in view of the lines along which canon law has evolved during the past three centuries, it is paradoxically true that, if he were alive now, St Vincent de Paul would no less energetically repeat, "You are not laywomen, you are religious".

Actually, though it has always remained true that their "monastery is the sick-room, their chapel the parish church, their cloister the streets of the city, their enclosure obedience, their grille the fear of God and their veil holy modesty", the hundreds of thousands of members of the "little company" have never belonged to the world, despite appearances to the contrary. The same sort of bold initiative which made them do away with the grilles generally imposed by the Council of Trent made them adopt the custom of making simple, annual vows. Their vows are not perpetual—though many similar Congregations based on the Vincentian spirit make perpetual vows—not so that they may give up a life of endless sacrifice to the demands of charity, but so that the regular renewal of their vows will also mean a renewal of their fervour in responding to those demands. Like the reception of candidates and the clothing of novices, the taking of vows among the Daughters of Charity[1] is of the utmost simplicity.

[1] St Vincent de Paul called the Congregation *Filles de la Charité* ("Daughters of Charity") but in English-speaking countries they are often known as Sisters of Charity.

In their motherhouse in Paris, where Our Lady of the Miraculous Medal appeared to Sister Catherine Labouré (who kept her secret for forty years as she continued her work of taking care of the aged sick), Daughters of Charity are trained, not by the dozen, but by hundreds and, what is really remarkable, this "mass production" of sisters produces religious who are docile, skilful and perfectly balanced. The Sister Directrice at the motherhouse has a few Vincentian Fathers and a few of her sisters in religion to assist her in a task which, elsewhere, would be considered impossible. But she trains large groups of girls from every walk of life in every country to be authentic Daughters of Charity, basing their lives on a tradition and spirit which has as its fundamental principle never to seek or ask for anything extra nor to request dispensation of any kind.

Once a girl has been trained so that she no longer thinks "as the world thinks", she is sent out to teach catechism. But surely they must be well trained themselves before they are able to teach the Faith to others? One Sister Servant, as their superiors are called, explained that the service of the poor and constant contact with Christ in prayer gradually and effortlessly supply this training.

How is a genuine vocation to the Daughters of Charity distinguished? Basically, a young woman who wants to join the Congregation must be willing to become mother, sister and daughter of the poorest, most gravely sick and most miserable of God's creatures.

The history of charitable works is studded with the names of many Sisters of Charity, some of them the daughters of noble and aristocratic families, others the children of ordinary working people. They were among the first women religious to go to the missions, pioneered in the field of social work, collaborated in the founding and early days of the Red Cross, from its beginnings on the battlefield at Solferino, where their work paralleled Florence Nightingale's. As St Vincent de Paul told them, their lives must be a constant mirroring of Christ's life, and so the only limits that their charity knows are those which would distract them from God's presence among the poor and wretched.

CHAPTER IX

SOME FACTORS IN CONVENT LIFE

WOMEN RELIGIOUS AND FREEDOM OF CONSCIENCE

Superiors and mistresses of novices are forbidden by canon law to demand, or even to make it in any way obligatory, that their subjects render them a "manifestation of conscience". The older Orders and Congregations, which formerly obliged their subjects to such an account by rule, rescinded the obligation when the code was published.

"Manifestation of conscience" applies to the "internal forum", that is, everything which goes on within a nun's soul. Like every other Catholic, but generally more frequently and with great care and completeness, every woman religious accuses herself before her confessor of all her sins and faults through word, deed, thought or omission. She begs pardon for external faults from her superior, or her sisters in religion, during the spiritual exercise generally called the *culpa* or "chapter of faults", though some institutes make provision for a different procedure. The slight "penances" which a nun is given at the confession of her fault are meritorious and educative satisfactions which, despite modern literature's attempts to dramatize them, are usually quite commonplace and ordinary.

A sister is not obliged to reveal her temptations to her

superior or confessor, nor need she give any account of her "lights" in prayer, unless of course, in either case, she is urged thereto by the Holy Spirit.

The local bishop appoints the convent's ordinary confessor, who has no external authority over the community. Every three months, another confessor, who is called the "extraordinary" confessor, visits the convent. In addition, women religious who are not members of an enclosed community may make their confession to any priest in any church they may pass; if they are enclosed they have the right to request the occasional help of another confessor. According to canon 611, any sister may also hand to her local superior sealed letters for the bishop or the superior general.

The Church has, thus, taken every possible precaution to prevent abuse of conscience in religious communities of women. It sometimes used to happen that some superiors, though their motives were of the highest, would be impelled by a too-inquisitive solicitude to demand that their subjects tell them everything. Thus, in an age when most young women were raised in a family atmosphere which allowed them all too little initiative, the remnants of independence which they possessed on their entrance into religion would be destroyed by a domineering and demanding superior.

Some people, however, might feel that what we have seen is merely a reaction from one abuse to another, so that now the religious life is merely a community of individuals living together in external submission to their rules and customs, with a superior at their head whose job it is to make sure that this external discipline, at least, is respected. But this attitude overlooks the fact that a religious community's rule influences its members' souls as much as, if not more than, it does the actions and deportment of their bodies. Besides, the limits which canon law puts on a superior's discretion need not affect her intuition and knowledge of souls and God's way with souls. Prayer must be the basis of her counsel and direction, which should be after the pattern of God's patience.

It is in the ordinary way of things in the religious life that a subject will frequently receive grace and knowledge in talks with her superior. On the other hand, it frequently happens that a sister will have nothing to say to "Mother"—which, in many cases, is an indication that everything is under control in that area, that human failings are fighting a losing battle against regular prayer and the sacraments.

TALENTS AND THE RELIGIOUS LIFE

In the religious life, natural talents, of course, are less important than the supernatural virtues. At the same time, it is not necessarily true that every talented young woman will sacrifice her capabilities for ever the moment she enters religion. Naturally, as a religious, her first duty is to become a *good* religious—but it not infrequently happens that the exercise of her talents helps her to achieve that end more quickly and efficiently.

St Teresa of Avila, for example, was able to combine a life of intimate mystical union with writing books which have given her a place of eminence among foremost Spanish authors. And those two Catherines, of Alexandria and of Siena, were holy and talented enough not only to become two of the Church's greatest saints, but in their lifetimes to have formed around themselves groups which included some of the greatest minds of their times. St Teresa of Lisieux's *Autobiography* is not only a testimony of God's grace and love, it is also something of a "best seller", because of its author's simplicity and directness of style.

But in all these cases, successful development of a natural talent was not something which was deliberately aimed at. It came as a natural consequence of the spiritual axiom that says that supernatural grace and natural talents will balance one another, so that neither will be hindered, in a prudent soul, by the other. There are other cases, however, in which grace seems to confer on a soul which is not especially talented gifts which are out of the ordinary and generally associated with individuals of high talent and capability.

In the long run, of course, the answer to how and if a religious should make use of her natural talents lies in the fact that her first "professional" duty is her own sanctification, and prayer and work for the sanctification of the whole world. But is that any different from every Christian duty? Certainly not —except that a lay person will also have one or more other professions, while holiness is really a religious's "business". Lay people may put off the business of holiness until a later date, when, they feel, they will be able to give it the attention it demands; a religious begins to deal with it immediately, as work marked "Urgent".

In the past, many superiors felt that the fact that their institute's basic end was holiness made it permissible for them to change and move about their sisters without being sure that they had training suitable for the various undertakings to which they were sent; after all, they reasoned, it is more important for Sister to be a good religious than a good nurse (teacher, social worker, etc.). Nowadays, the situation is different, and not many superiors would think of sending a sister to a particular post without being sure that she was suited to the work and, if not already trained, capable of learning the necessary skills with ease and proficiency.

Bureaucracy, in its own way, has had considerable influence in this area. In some places, government offices have required all teachers to be certificated, or to hold a degree or a diploma. As a result, many middle-aged sisters, because such certificates were not necessary in their younger days, find that, after twenty or thirty years of teaching, they are no longer considered adequately trained for their work. Many of them have had to be removed from teaching posts and found other work.

They go on praying and loving, however, and consider their removal as only another God-sent opportunity to practise self-denial: "They are my mother and my sister and my brother, who do the will of my Father who is in heaven."

FRIENDS AND FRIENDSHIP

No reflective, serious-minded laywoman could ever deny a woman religious her rights to be called "Sister" or "Mother" (the custom of calling the members of some institutes "Madame" is, fortunately, dying out). Women religious have not simply appropriated to themselves these names which combine respect and diffidence with affection. They are, in fact, mothers and sisters, but in much the same way as our Lady, the "world's first religious" was, who, as mother and virgin, gave herself and all she had to the whole world without asking or expecting anything in return.

A woman religious's obligation to avoid manifesting (or feeling) any preference among her sisters, pupils or patients, to avoid giving any unseemly signs of even legitimate affection, and to keep herself from being a screen between God and souls demands tact, so that she will not become inhuman, and vigilance, lest she become too human. It is frequently sufficient at the outset to explain the whole situation to her superior for the difficulty to be cleared up, and the snare exposed and avoided. Nevertheless, the very highest motives will often disguise the real character of an affection which is too natural and could lead to difficulty.

Too frequently, for example, a sister will become the focus around which a conflict revolves between her institute and, say, a group of her pupils' mothers, who insist that Sister is not enough appreciated by her superior and that "it is about time something was done". In such a situation, the sister herself may ask to be sent out of the area, or her superiors, without consulting her, may decide to do it. Immediately, her well-intentioned but misguided champions raise the alarm. Someone mentions a petition. Even the parish priest may be drawn into the conflict: "Ah well, you know how these sisters are; they're the same everywhere. And it won't do any good to bring the bishop into it because, as soon as he tries to do anything about what has happened, mother general will hide behind her council and say that they have been thinking about withdrawing all their sisters from the diocese. And he will be unable to accept that. . . ." And so it goes on, with Sister leaving and a replacement being sent. At first, there is strangeness and awkwardness, but things quickly settle down and the whole incident is forgotten.

In a word, women religious deal with their own affections according to St Paul's description of charity in his letter to the Corinthians. They supernaturalize their human love, and thereby produce an emotion and affection which knows no favourites, never demands a return and is always ready to sacrifice itself. Because it is not directed towards any particular person, a religious's life is available to everyone and, because of its detachment, so grows that it seems inexhaustible, able to extend to an entire ward of sick and aged people, or a whole class of young children. Because it is not based on purely human tendencies, it extends even to the maimed, the disfigured, the seriously ill. It penetrates human appearances to find Christ whom, above and in all, it loves.

Teaching sisters, of course, have many opportunities for forming useful and well-ordered friendships with their pupils. Nine out of ten of their students will leave school and that will be the last anyone will hear of them, but there is always the one student who becomes a faithful correspondent, reporting events in her family life, the birth of her children, and so forth. Eventually the children return to study at the school and they, in their turn, carry on their friendship and initiate new ones of their own.

Analogous to this situation is the friendly loyalty pupils of one or another Congregation retain all through their lives and wherever they may be. It is not unusual for a sister in a strange city to be greeted by a girl whom she has never seen or met before but who has been taught by other members of her Congregation.

Within the community, friendship is always built and maintained upon a strong basis of fraternal charity. Superiors must pay discreet attention to the friendships within the community, disciplining any faults or failures as soon as they develop. On another level, it is comforting for a religious to live surrounded by souls in the state of grace after spending a long working-day in the world, where so many people with whom she comes into contact are, perhaps, far from that state. Their mutual affection will only rarely be expressed or manifested, but the fraternal embrace on a feast day, for instance, becomes the more meaningful for that.

Though it seems strange to point it out, perhaps, one of the most patent signs of the depth of the affection within a religious community is the notice of the last hours and death of a sister sent out to other houses of the Congregation after her death. A sister dies surrounded by her sisters, encouraged by their prayers and affection, mourned by their unabashed tears. In religion, people love one another just as though they were all members of the same family—which, in fact, they are.

But what of their own, natural, families? Must religious stop loving their relations once they enter religion? Sometimes, families feel that they have been deserted and robbed of their daughters' love. The fact is, of course, that God rewards them more than they can imagine for sacrificing their child and her affection to him. Within the necessary limits imposed by religious life and its spirit of detachment, sisters have far less contact with their families than would other young women living away from home. It used to be the case, when family relations were far more formal and rigid than they are nowadays anyway, that religious would barely have any contact with their relations. (Such was the case, in the days, for instance, of Fr Rodriguez, S.J., whose spiritual treatises have been the bane of many a novice's life for the past three centuries, and who considered it virtuous not to write to his mother for the first twenty years of his religious life. After that time, he wrote a long and rambling letter in which he described to her all the great events of his life as a religious.) Nowadays, things are more liberally arranged: letters or a visit once a month, except during Lent and Advent, is more or less the general rule, though some older groups hold on to their traditional regulations. And what about letters? Do superiors still read them before they are posted, and before the incoming ones are distributed? Yes—when they have time. Besides, many superiors have found that reading these letters (which is their privilege and, in some Congregations, their duty) is an excellent way of keeping track of all the influences on the souls of their subjects. Also, it often happens that a young postulant or novice will find it easier to write to her family about the things which are disturbing her than it would be to tell them to her superior who is, after all, still a relative stranger to her.

Suppose their parents fall sick or grow too old to take care of themselves, and there is no other child who can care for them? Except in those Orders of nuns who are restricted to their enclosure by the solemn vows they have made, it is more and more becoming the practice of religious Congregations to allow their members to return home for a short time when illness or death makes their presence necessary or desirable. Rome is becoming increasingly generous in granting this permission, which used to be restricted to certain nursing Congregations.

Not long ago, the Little Sisters of Jesus began to make arrangements for a house for the aged or sick parents of some of their members. Surely this is an idea which other communities might consider and imitate, since it is so much in the spirit of the fourth commandment, which the life of the evangelical counsels does not, of course, abrogate.

Rome seems more doubtful, however, about the convalescent visits to their families which members of certain Congregations are allowed to make when they become ill or seriously fatigued. A sister in such a condition could hardly edify by her faithful observance of the rule (an observance which may have been modified precisely because of her condition), and she is scarcely well protected against the atmosphere of the world. Those in a position best to judge and decide seem to feel that it would be better for such sisters to recuperate in another convent of their own Congregation.

CHAPTER X

DIFFICULTIES OF HEALTH AND AGE

No woman whose health is not strong, or who is already past young womanhood, need feel that, despite the attraction she feels for the religious life, her condition or age would prevent her from entering a convent. There are, fortunately, many Congregations which accept candidates whose health or age might be an impediment to their joining other groups. It remains true, naturally, that, though weak health or advanced age no longer need be impediments to the religious life, great reserves of courage, patience and generosity, coupled with sound judgement and a sense of humour, are indispensable to such a vocation.

In 1930, a young Polish woman, now Mother Marie des Douleurs, founded the Institute of Jesus Crucified, to "make the religious life available to women who are sick, invalided, or of weak health". The Congregation includes sisters who are deaf, blind, diabetic, asthmatic and paralysed. Some of the members have made their vows lying in the beds from which they would probably not rise for the rest of their lives. The spirit of the group is summed up in the two words of its motto: "Amen, Alleluia". Sisters of Jesus Crucified lead an essentially contemplative life and do only such work as is compatible with this life and their state of health. They are bound to simple enclosure, and have no lay-sisters, though there is a group of secular oblates and a union of the sick attached to the Congregation for lay-people who wish to join their own prayers and sufferings to the work of the sisters. In addition to its four convents in France, the Institute has a convent in England, and two in the United States.

There are two Congregations in Italy which accept blind candidates: the Sisters of Adoration, at Milan, who were founded by Don Orione, and the Daughters of Christ the King, who are a dependent group of the Poor Daughters of St Cajetan. All the members of these Congregations are blind, and live a contemplative life according to a rule especially adapted to their condition. The Sisters of St Paul, at Paris, accept one blind candidate for every two sighted members of the community.

In Rome, the Salesian Sisters of the Sacred Hearts have three members who are deaf mutes. Similar provision is made by the Institute of Sisters of Our Lady of the Seven Dolours, and the Daughters of Wisdom, in France, have a group of deaf-mute oblates connected with their Congregation. The Sisters of Our Lady of Calvary, a Brazilian Congregation, have also organized a dependent group for deaf candidates.

In Colombia, the Italian Salesian, Fr Louis Variazia, whose cause for beatification has been introduced, founded a Congregation for lepers and the daughters of lepers. The Canadian Daughters-Réparatrices of the Sacred Heart live according to a rule especially devised to make the religious life possible for young women of weak health. In France, the Little Servants of the Lamb of God, who are members of a pious union, have thirteen convents, and one hundred and fifty members, all of whom are handicapped in some way. Young women who, despite poor health, feel themselves called to the contemplative life, may apply for admission to the Benedictine Priory of Peace, or to the Dominican Sisters of Our Lady.

It is not surprising, of course, that these Congregations which accept young women who are handicapped or in weak health do not, on the other hand, accept older women. The obvious difficulties connected with a religious community composed entirely or in great part of invalids cannot be increased beyond prudence or discretion.

The age limits for candidates to groups of religious women vary a great deal. Many institutes take candidates who are not younger than eighteen, and not older than thirty, in some cases thirty-five. This admission depends upon the applicant's being in sound health and showing the usual signs of religious vocation, and upon there being a sound and sufficient reason for delayed application—usually family responsibilities. (Many experts in this field agree that a "delayed" vocation has a greater chance of persevering than a "late" vocation.)

Some of the more austere Orders and Congregations delay the age of admission until twenty-one; the Cistercians' life, for example, demands a mature and balanced personality, if the candidate is to adapt herself with a minimum of difficulty to the austerity of their life, especially their silence. In some cases, after examination, women who are older than thirty are accepted by the Carmelites, Visitation nuns and Poor Clares, all of whom sometimes accept candidates who have passed their fortieth birthday.

Present changes and development in the status of "extern sisters" promise to make the religious life even more generally available to older or less robust women. Sharing in the life of their community, but absolved from its more austere burdens, they are no less religious and have equal opportunities for devotion and sacrifice.

At the end of the *Guide to the Catholic Sisterhoods in the United States*, there is a note which it may be helpful to repeat here: "Women or girls who have been unsuccessful in finding a community which will accept them, because of some difficulty (age, birth, marriage or health), should write to the author: Fr Thomas P. McCarthy, C.S.V., or to the Rev. Jean-Marie J. Bauchet, Ph.D., Chaplain of Providence House, 73 Vernon Street, Worcester, Massachusetts." In England, information in great abundance is made available by the Daughters of Our Lady of Good Counsel, Vocation House, Hallaton, Market Harborough, Leics., who will supply information concerning any Order or Congregation in particular, and the religious life for women in general.

Such centres of information would probably be of great assistance everywhere, to counsel and advise women who feel themselves called to the religious life but who, for one reason or another, anticipate or actually have difficulty in finding a Congregation to which they are adapted and which will accept them. The question of age, it seems, still needs a great deal of reconsideration. Nowadays, women of thirty, forty or fifty are as mature, but not as "old", as women of their years would have been, say, a hundred years ago. Modern life and its conveniences make it possible for all of us to preserve greater quantities of energy for a longer, and more useful, life. Besides, in most cases, a vocation which has been delayed has been nourished while the individual carried on a profession or a career, looking forward to the time when she would be able and free to enter religion, and at the same time developing skills, and wisdom and sound judgement which will serve both herself and her eventual religious family in good stead. It is cruelly disappointing to many women to find themselves rejected by one religious community after another because they are too old—after having lived their lives with probably no less devotion and dedication to Christ than a woman already under vows.

Legislation which lays down the minimum age for candidates for Congregations of religious women at fifteen to eighteen applies to the religious life strictly so-called; thus, many Congregations have juniorates, where young girls of eleven to thirteen are given remote preparation for the religious life. Their studies are adapted to their own age-level, just as they would be in an ordinary school, and their introduction to the ideals and customs of the religious life is gradual. They are not expected to commit themselves in any way to the religious life and may, of course, leave the juniorate whenever they please. Under this system, many Congregations have been able to enrol members and re-open convents and schools which, for lack of adequate staff, had had to be closed. Some people object to the juniorate system on the grounds that many of the girls, after having been educated and trained at the expense of the Congregation, leave without going on to postulancy and novitiate. Most superiors, however, feel that the opportunity their Congregation has had to form young women to be solid Christians, with a knowledge of the true spirit of prayer and a consciousness of the duties of a Christian, far outweighs the financial disadvantage involved. Besides, they say, many of those girls have daughters—or even grand-daughters—who return and follow on with a religious vocation.

CHAPTER XI

THE RELIGIOUS HABIT

A religious Congregation's custom-book is a practical and well worked-out scheme for putting the Rule into practice. It is more fluid and flexible than the Rule, of course, and may vary according to the particular country or region in which a particular group is living the Rule.

Despite its flexibility, the custom-book inevitably includes many prescriptions which do not change according to time or place. Some counsels and suggestions are just as wise in modern twentieth-century life as they were a hundred, or even three hundred, years ago. A Rule which is applied by thousands of consecrated souls over a long period of time is bound to generate traditions which are perfectly adapted and proportioned to its spirit. On the other hand, there are some passages in a custom-book which no longer have any real sense or reason, and are obviously the remains of a past generation and attitude. Retention of these outmoded customs betrays a kind of unthinking formalism and loyalty to the letter, rather than the spirit, of the Rule.

Many Congregations, however, hesitate to change their custom-book in the slightest, and continue to be genuinely inconvenienced by prescriptions which were laid down for life in another century. Eventually, the inconvenience and reluctance to assume responsibility for changing the custom-book comes to the attention of authorities, who calm their conscience and direct that certain changes be made.

Most frequently, changes and adaptations in Congregations

of women religious have to do with their religious habit, which is, strictly speaking, usually prescribed in detail not by the custom-book but by the Rule itself. Because the habit is part of the Rule, it is understandable that there be even greater reluctance to change or modify it. Some women religious today find themselves bound, for example, to adjust their veil, every time they put it on, with a pin or a complicated arrangement of pins and folds—whereas a few stitches with needle and thread would arrange it once and for all in the required manner and save time and trouble. Several superiors have, at one time or another, attempted to initiate changes in the question of the habit and its style, but have been thwarted by the loyalty and stubborn devotion of their subjects.

On the other hand, though there can be little question that some religious habits are outmoded to the extent that wearing them is an inconvenience and mortification not even foreseen by the founder or foundress, it is nevertheless true that some attempts at modification, and "modernization", of the habit have ended in a garment which will soon be no less outmoded and look as, if not more, old-fashioned than the one it replaces. Surely there is a great deal to say for a long and gracefully folded skirt which lends an air of dignity and calm to even the most ill-favoured woman! And can there be much foresight in a change which does away with a complicated headdress and substitutes for it a construction which makes its wearer look like a social worker of a past generation?

Unimportant though the whole question may seem at first, it is basically quite a serious one, especially when feminine psychology is taken into account. Women religious are not, except in some groups with specialized apostolates, supposed to look like lay-women—because they are not lay-women. To adapt their habit, therefore, so that they look more like dowdy lay-women than religious in uniform seems to serve no purpose whatever.

It is interesting to notice that those habits worn by religious women which were initially designed precisely as religious garb (and not, for instance, in imitation of an Italian widow's mourning weeds, or a French châtelaine's working costume) have endured longest in their original design with the least inconvenience to their wearers and the least need for modification. Habits worn by the Benedictines, Dominicans, Poor Clares and Carmelites, for example, are monastic in origin and were, from the very beginning, meant as the "uniform" of women consecrated to God. On the other hand, almost every habit which, in the beginning, had as one of its features a sweeping choir-train, or a complicated headdress, or an intricately (and sometimes symbolically) pleated skirt, has had to be modified, quite frequently in exactly that feature which made it so distinctive.

From a practical point of view, one cannot help wondering about the risks some sisters must take when travelling about in our busy, traffic-filled cities when, because of their headdresses, they cannot possibly see in any direction except directly in front of them. It would also be interesting to read the conclusions of, say, a member of a medical or nursing Congregation who had examined sisters whose heads are swathed in yards and layers of material in all weather, indoors and out. Would they indicate, perhaps, that there is another cause, for example, of a sister's headache other than hard work alone?

Surely a guiding principle in this entire question of religious habits, and their reform and modification, is that the dramatic and striking should always be avoided, and that any feature which becomes inconvenient, outmoded or even, perhaps, ridiculous, should be done away with. On this same subject, it is also encouraging to see that many Congregations which have not yet gone as far as doing away with the separate grade of lay-sister have at least decided that there should no longer be a distinction between the habit worn by choir religious and that worn by lay-sisters. After all, a religious habit is a sacramental, and there should be nothing about it, or the way in which it must be worn, to detract from its religious character and dignity. Nor, on the other hand, should it be allowed simply to degenerate into a uniform, thereby losing much or all of its implications of dedication and consecration.

CHAPTER XII

IN THE WORLD, BUT NOT OF THE WORLD...

As a prelude to the next chapter, in which Secular Institutes are discussed, it may be well to say a few words about the religious life properly so called (or, at least, as distinct from the religious life as led by members of Secular Institutes) and the relations existing between religious and the world, between themselves and the people with and for whom they work. One of the merits of the Secular Institutes is the opportunity they afford for satisfying a vocation which, for various internal or external reasons, cannot be fulfilled in the conditions of more or less complete withdrawal from the world associated with the life of members of active, contemplative or mixed Congregations.

Abnegation means denial, negation of oneself. No one would say, of course, that religious have a monopoly of self-denial. Not only consecrated laywomen, but even mothers and spinsters, though they have not made the vows of religious, devote themselves entirely and without stint to their families or some other group, and are frequently called to an entire self-forgetfulness and an admirable heroism. Members of Secular Institutes continue to live in the world as part of their vocation and are able to take advantage of certain of the benefits of living in the world. The external liberty which they are allowed, and which is necessary if they are to act, without attracting attention, as the "leaven", guarantees them a certain minimum of independence of action, even though their private or semi-public vows, and the secret obligations imposed upon them by their way of life, add to the responsibilities already inherent in their professional life or career. They keep their own names, and the ownership, if not the free use, of their own property, including their talents. Dedicated *ex professo* to a life of service and apostolic work, they must always be able and free to exercise all their capabilities to the highest degree. One of their chief preoccupations is so to become part of their milieu, and so to share in all the world's sufferings and pain, that they will be able quickly and directly to bring to it the comfort and encouragement of Christ's presence. They must be outstanding not only because of their high degree of virtue, but also because of their skill and professional capability.

Surely there is nothing "imperfect" in a life like that. On the contrary, the Church has designated such a life a "state of perfection". But—and it is as well to make the point at the outset—what makes Secular Institutes different from religious Congregations is not merely that their members need not live in community, either because of professional obligations, family responsibilities, or independence of character, but that their renunciation of self, their abnegation, has a slightly different meaning than that of a religious.

A consecrated laywoman gives herself along with everything else she gives to her neighbour: she *is* and *owns* what she gives. A religious, on the other hand, empties herself and her work entirely of her "self": nothing she has or does should be referable to herself, but to Christ, in whom she can and does "do all things". Beginning with the day on which she makes her vows, and increasingly daily all through her life, her attitude must always be St Paul's: "I live now, not I, but Christ lives in me". Having died to the world—to the extent that, with her final vows, she makes her last will and testament—she places herself, her talents and all she is or has in the hands of her superiors, for them to govern and direct as

God's personal property. Parallel with this entire commitment, there is a freedom from responsibility in these matters which arises from the fact that she is protected from a superior's excessive authoritarianism by the laws of the Church, to which superiors are always answerable for the disposition of their subjects' talents and energies.

Henceforth her spiritual life is safeguarded once and for all against anything prejudicial to its growth in holiness and union; nothing, neither misunderstanding, pettiness, nor incorrect spiritual or medical diagnosis, can seriously or permanently prejudice her life. Crucified, like her divine Spouse, she shares in the work of redemption to the extent that she allows herself to be used as an instrument. It may seem that what she does is ineffective and that her talents are being improperly used or not used at all; actually, her effectiveness can no longer be gauged according to natural criteria. Sometimes, even superiors, otherwise known as wise and discerning, and directors, who have been successful in guiding other souls along the higher ways of the spiritual life, will miss the point of a particular sister's life, and it will only be at the Last Day, when all things are made known, that everyone will understand what our Lord meant when he said to a Poor Clare of Jerusalem: "The religious life is so splendid a thing that, if a postulant should die even after having spent a very few days in religion, her union with divine charity in Eternity will be much greater than it would have been had she remained in the world. She has been away from the world for only a few days, but already her spirit is separated from it by a deep and wide chasm, because she made the interior gift of her liberty to me."

The unconditional self-surrender is a stumbling-block and a scandal to the spirit of the modern world because so many people find surrender of one's liberty even more incomprehensible than self-denial and control of the senses. On the other hand, the conviction that God has called her to make precisely this sacrifice and to prefer him above everything else, and the knowledge that the sacrifice has been made freely and deliberately, should be, and usually is, enough to make any woman religious content with the life she has committed herself to.

Despite all we have said thus far, it remains true that a contemplative religious is, perhaps, more fortunate than her active sisters. The contemplative's approach to God is direct, and she more easily avoids the tension which can develop not because of responsibility to one's neighbours, which no Christian can escape, but because of administrative affairs, State controls and "minimum requirements", and the demands and expectations of the world. It has happened, of course, that periods of restriction and subjection have produced greater progress than could have been expected. Even persecutions, which made work in one locality or branch of the apostolate impossible, have done good by turning a Congregation's attention to another field, in which they were eventually to do even greater and more extensive work. The main point is that there should be no limits placed upon a religious's availability.

CHAPTER XIII

THE SECULAR INSTITUTES

What are Secular Institutes? "Associations of clerics or lay-people whose members, the better to advance in Christian perfection and devote themselves entirely to the apostolate, dedicate themselves to practising the counsels of the Gospels while continuing to live in the world."[1] Why were they organized and given juridical recognition as "states of perfection" by the Church? "Because their members, although living in the world, have completely consecrated themselves to God and the good of souls with the Church's approval: and further, because, in different ways and to varying degrees, they all have an internal hierarchic organization."

Pius XII gave the Secular Institutes official recognition on February 2nd, 1947 in the papal constitution *Provida Mater*, which put forth the Church's mind on what such associations should be and how they should be organized, and which was implemented on March 12th, 1948 by the *Motu proprio, Primo Feliciter*.

Publication of these two documents brought to light a multitude of souls hidden with Christ in God, who courageously and with great spirit are striving to reach sanctity while living in the world, and who had previously been almost unknown because they did not have juridical status.

In the following year, Pius XII expressed his great satisfaction at this spontaneous growth and underlined the Secular

[1] See, in this series, volume 87 (English edn, 86), *Secular Institutes*, by Gabriel Reidy, O.F.M.

Institutes' mission of being "salt, light and leaven, always and everywhere at work, living as part of every class of men, from the most humble to the highest, and striving by their word, example and every human means to reach these others and influence their lives, so that finally the whole mass will be leavened and rise until it is entirely Christ".

We must notice at the outset, however, that though Secular Institutes are built on the basis of the evangelical counsels—poverty, chastity and obedience—and though their members are genuinely committed to live within these virtues by vows, oaths or promises which bind them to consecrate their whole beings and lives to the apostolate, community life is not an essential part of their structure. This is true though it may happen that some members of a workers' Congregation, for example, will live together, and despite the fact that some central residence, or motherhouse, for the entire Institute is generally, though not necessarily, provided as a training centre for candidates. It also serves as a place where members who are sick, aged, or with some difficulty arising from health, social position or of a more purely spiritual nature, may go to benefit by that fraternal hospitality implied by the idea of a family, religious or secular.

Members of Secular Institutes are not bound to wear any distinctive habit. In most instances, as a matter of fact, it would not be desirable or possible. Several of the Institutes have various devices which are more a help to their members' recognizing one another than anything else: the Theresians wear a cleverly designed bracelet, members of other Institutes may wear a simple crucifix or medal around their necks, while others have nothing to distinguish themselves from ordinary lay-people beyond the mantles or veils which all members wear in chapel. We shall examine below the reasons behind this reluctance for any distinguishing habit or apparel.

On the other hand, members should, obviously, dress quite simply and modestly—without, however, going to the extreme of attracting attention by their plainness. In one Institute, the members must always wear long sleeves, but need not wear stockings. This is not as strange as it may seem, however: first of all, wearing long sleeves during a hot summer could be made a small penance for indecency of dress at bathing beaches. Besides, going without stockings saves more than money: it saves the time which mending them would take. And a member of a Secular Institute cannot call her time her own—it belongs to her neighbour.

Though this question of dress or habit is indifferent in itself, still, the feminine psychology can sometimes dwell on it so that very real problems, perhaps even scruples, can grow out of it. And it is precisely here that, kindly and graciously, obedience steps in to solve the problem: one consults one's superiors and submits to their decision. Even in Secular Institutes this is true.

In an area like this, though, a person must always use a little common sense—and have a sense of humour. Suppose a member of a Secular Institute, which has members working on several social levels, happens to notice that another member has a fur coat, given to her, say, by her family. What should she think? Her first thought should be that her sister member has already consulted superiors, discussed the matter with them, and would not be wearing the coat without their permission and counsel. This spontaneous fraternal charity demands a high degree of virtue, naturally, but, after all, a member of a Secular Institute *is supposed* to strive after heroic virtue.

Some Institutes handle the matter of who should wear what sort of clothing very simply: after a holiday, whatever clothing the members have been given by friends or families is pooled. Anything which is surplus to one member's requirements is given to another, perhaps less fortunate, member.

The discretion or secrecy which many Secular Institutes preserve about their private consecration is not merely a matter of secrecy for its own sake. After all, the real courage in leading a life of heroic virtue is not in its publication or time-table, but in the spirit with which one remains faithful to it surrounded by a world whose paganism runs counter to it. The need is for consecrated people who will infiltrate and occupy the secularist areas of society without drawing attention to themselves by any external sign, and gradually and quietly introduce the presence of God.

In any case, this "pious anonymity" is not a twentieth-century idea: the Daughters of the Heart of Mary, founded during the French Revolution and who wear no religious habit, were for a time forbidden to reveal even to their close relatives that they were religious.

What sort of apostolic work do members of Secular Institutes do? Before moving on to the specialized nature of their apostolate, it may be as well to examine first precisely that point of their vocation which seems, at first glance, least apostolic but which is, in a sense, their most peculiarly apostolic feature: the apostolate of their own social class or circle, which they sanctify through their work or profession. Career, profession, work—they are all, in one sense, perfectly indifferent provided they are pursued in a spirit of charity and detachment. For example, if one more consecrated nurse or teacher goes to work in an area or among a social class which is already infused with Christian principles, so much the better; even though, without her, the people in the area would still remain true Christians.

On the other hand, it is obvious how much real worth and value there is in a situation in which, say, a dancer, who works hard to become *première danseuse* by disciplining her body, has already consecrated that body and the soul informing it to God, in secret, and brings backstage with her, and into the practice halls, the spirit and love of Christ. Or consider the great good which could be done to this modern world of ours by a woman whose career is politics—but whose career as a politician is based and rests on her secret life as a consecrated member of a Secular Institute.

Whether a woman is a dancer, a politician, a lawyer, or

simply a typist or bus conductress, the essential thing is that, as a member of a Secular Institute, she brings the presence of God and his charity, incarnate in herself, along with her wherever she goes or works. And part of her vocation will be to be competent at her work, to gain respect by earning her wages and knowing her job.

Surely, though, any married or single woman could do all this? Certainly—and the activity of such women is generally described by two words which are so vitally important in the modern Church: Catholic Action. But a married woman's first obligation is to her home and family. Above and before anything else, she belongs to her husband and her children, while "the virgin looks to the things of God, that she may be healthy in body and spirit".

A member of a Secular Institute, therefore, has time to spend on her neighbour who is, for her, Christ himself. She is free to overlook, or at least not worry about, reward, since Christ himself is her reward as she tends the sick, or prepares a brief, or looks after children, or, skilfully and tactfully, turns a conversation from frivolous small talk to truth and charity, or has coffee after the theatre and brings the fruit of her prayer and reading to bear on a discussion of the real meaning of the play she and her companion have just seen. And when she returns to her home, she knows that Christ is waiting there for her. If it is late, she knows that her sisters in convents have long since retired, and she prepares herself for sleep by adoring that one Spouse whom they all serve and to whom they are all consecrated.

Leading a life like this, in which she is so much in the world, it is almost inevitable that a member of a Secular Institute should encounter situations which try and test her courage and even, perhaps, her perseverance. What safeguard has she? She is protected by the commitments she has made which have released her from considerations of herself and her own desires, and by her rule which, flexible and adaptable though it may be, is unswerving in its direction, demands absolute obedience, and for whose observance she is answerable to her superiors. Without this hard core of regularity she will not be a professional striver after perfection, but an amateur, a spiritual dilettante.

The Church, naturally, continues to encourage and praise the individual and private pursuit of perfection, and considers the evergrowing seriousness of many laypeople in striving after holiness an encouraging and blessed phenomenon. But she has already given juridical recognition to the idea of Secular Institutes in general, and to some particular Institutes, because she considers it highly opportune and suitable that members of Secular Institutes bind themselves to their organizations as strongly as members of the older Orders and Congregations do to theirs. The Institute, in this way, is able to make free and complete use of a member's life and talents, for the service of God, and, reciprocally, leaves itself unfailingly at his service for counsel and aid. Thus, the commitments between the Institute and its members are mutual, and guarantee permanency as they increase effectiveness. This is also the reason why these commitments should be perpetual, at least on the part of the individual making them.

In 1957, it was announced in connection with the Congress of the States of Perfection, held at Rome, that at that time forty-nine Secular Institutes had been approved, of which thirteen were of pontifical jurisdiction, while the rest were of diocesan jurisdiction. These already approved Institutes were a part of the 197 groups which were seeking approbation. (It was said that many of the groups which had not yet been approved would be in time, after they had been able to profit by advice and experience in creating a stable organization.) The leaders among the approved Institutes were associations which pre-dated *Provida Mater*—some of them by twenty-five, thirty, or even fifty years.

Some Institutes have a branch for men and a separate branch for women. The Society of St Paul is one such group, and was founded in accordance with the advice and direction of Cardinal Ferrari; other groups with two distinct branches are the Missionaries of Christ the King, who were founded along Franciscan lines by Fr Agostino Gemelli, O.F.M., and Opus Dei, originally a Spanish institute which now has eighteen thousand members, of whom eight thousand are women, working all over the world. It is impossible, because some of the Secular Institutes insist so strongly on utmost privacy and secrecy, to give a complete list of all those which accept women.

The Grail, which is composed of women members only, was founded in the Netherlands, but now has many members in England and the United States. Its work includes the publication of Catholic literature, and activities in radio, theatre and television. At Loveland, Ohio, the institute has a centre where young women may stay to study the ideals of Christian womanhood and attend conferences on motherhood, the rôle of women in the professional world, and other pertinent subjects.

Some Secular Institutes concentrate on working for priests, as housekeepers, secretaries and so on. Other groups have been founded primarily for widows, in order to give such women the opportunity to consecrate their lives entirely to God while remaining in the world to work and meet family responsibilities. Finally, some already existing religious Congregations have adapted their tried and tested rule of life to the new states of perfection and have organized Secular Institutes constructed along lines similar in spirit to the mother-Congregation. The Fraternity of Jesus-Caritas, for example, is based on the spirit of Fr Charles de Foucauld which inspires the Little Sisters of Jesus, and the Sisters of Mary of the Catholic Apostolate have been given a way of life already associated with the Pallottine Fathers and Sisters.

In Canada, the Missionary Oblates of the Immaculate Conception were founded by the Oblates of Mary Immaculate. They already have groups in six countries and have more than a thousand members, all of whom are free to enter a religious Congregation. The Institute operates schools and study centres which prepare young women for the religious life.

The contemplative life has also inspired the foundation of some Secular Institutes. In 1923, the Missionaries of Our Lady of Mount Carmel were founded and, though they have no explicit connection with the Carmelite Order, their ideals, especially in everything which concerns devotion to our Lady, are the same. They do not accept widows as candidates and they solemnly promise to carry out the principal end of their Institute, which is to aid and assist priests wherever possible, especially in those places to which they do not have easy access.

Ten years later, Fr Marie-Eugène de l'Enfant Jésus, a Discalced Carmelite, founded the Institute of Notre-Dame de Vie, to make the contemplative life as accessible as possible to souls living in the world as witnesses of God. New members spend two years in a house of solitude, where they prepare themselves to live faithfully, in the world, the rule which obliges them to two hours of mental prayer daily, and the recitation of the Breviary. Once formed, members must spend forty-five days, which must include thirty consecutive days, out of every year at the house of solitude, and must spend a year there every twelve years. No matter what profession members follow after their initial formation, with the approval of their superiors, the basis of their apostolate is to give witness to God by their lives.

It becomes clear that Secular Institutes have been and will continue to be the answer to many of the problems hitherto connected with the life of a woman who, for one reason or another, could not enter religion nor be married. The consolation, encouragement and discipline of life implied by membership in a Secular Institute is an excellent counter-agent to the feelings of being wasted, misunderstood, exploited or loneliness which afflicted many, even privately consecrated, women before, and frequently resulted in bitterness and lack of effectiveness.

Another obvious advantage of these Institutes is that they have removed from the older Congregations and Orders the responsibility of accepting candidates, or work, which would be slightly less than entirely suitable and could have been a threat to the entire internal organization.

In his *Dialogues des Carmélites,* Bernanos caused the Prioress to say, "It is not the rule which protects us, but we who protect the rule". Whatever one may think of the book, the remark is certainly valid and authentic. Once a person has vowed to obey the rule, it must be obeyed, kept. If, after a while, it seems clear that some candidates cannot keep the rule without creating tensions in themselves—and their community—they should be advised to go elsewhere. It is also sensible to leave to others work which is not compatible with one's own Congregation's rule. Perhaps the initiative and fluidity of apostolate manifested by so many Secular Institutes will encourage some of the older Congregations to get rid of the accretions which their rule has developed since its first formulation and which seem to hinder their community's free activity. The final criterion must always be, however, the difference between a religious Congregation and a Secular Institute, and it is for each group to stick to its own last.

It sometimes seems that confessors, Catholic journalists and teachers are almost too eager in advising young people to apply as candidates for a Secular Institute. Secular Institutes need mature, balanced adults who are both sensitive to the needs of their neighbours in the world, and proof against the allure of a life in the world. Besides, and more generally speaking, a soul which despairs of saving itself in the world and rushes into any sort of consecrated life because it thinks it will be safer there, can hardly have reflected on the difficulty and sacrifice implicit in a life of dedication and self-effacement.

Yet there are some souls with genuine vocations which cannot be satisfied unless they have completely effaced themselves and surrendered entirely to God. In some cases, it will be necessary to carry out this donation in solitude and silence, and such a soul would, it seems, be better advised to enter a contemplative Congregation; others will need no less dedication and self-surrender, but may find working for their Spouse necessary as an externalization of their love, and for these life in an active Congregation seems advisable.

This is not, obviously, to minimize the need for and good work done by Secular Institutes who have, anyway, been approved and encouraged by Christ's Vicar. Nor is it meant to minimize the very real hazards to their spiritual life which they encounter daily and hourly, working as they do surrounded by the world and without even the protection of a religious habit. It is more difficult, perhaps, to be a soldier out of uniform, working behind enemy lines, than to be in the front line of fire, protected by communally built ramparts and encouraged by one's companions. The answer, perhaps, lies in each finding the best way to save her own soul—and the souls of others. Once that way has been found and chosen, however, there can be no looking back, nor envying others their freedom, or their lack of responsibility.

CHAPTER XIV

ADAPTATIONS

More and more during the past twenty-five years, adaptations in religious Congregations have gone further than a simple refashioning of the habit. They have involved some great and intricate problems, and have sometimes been recommended by the Church, influenced by changing times, and changes in the external forum have inevitably been felt in the internal forum. Because the most important adaptations have been made by superiors general in official meetings, with Rome's permission and encouragement, they have had more force and urgency. Most women religious, and especially their superiors, have welcomed the opportunity to make changes which, they feel, have increased the efficiency and power for good of their Congregations.

The changes have always been motivated by a desire to develop according to the growing and changing needs of the Church and the mystical body. Study groups, general meetings and discussion centres have all played a large part in facilitating an exchange of views and experience between women religious, and have, in some cases, shown the way to one Congregation or another. Regina Mundi, a theological institute at Rome which was founded to enable women religious to increase their theoretical and practical knowledge of theology, has also helped in this vital work of modernization. Religious meeting at this and other similar centres and conferences have come away more fully aware of the unity of the religious life, a unity which transcends Orders, Congregations and Rules, and have determined to do all they can to keep their particular group in step with the Church's progress. Superiors have been able to exchange experiences and have mutually benefited in acquiring greater knowledge of the problems encountered by modern candidates to religion.

In general, the tendency of these adaptations has been towards a greater simplicity of life, habit and daily schedule, with a great concentration on the necessity for a deep and solid spiritual training. As a result, many of the old-fashioned features of religious habits and customs have disappeared. Unions and associations of religious superiors have been set up so that superiors can remain in touch with one another and benefit by continuous mutual advice and counsel. Their contacts help them all to clear away the "dead wood" and allow the religious life to enjoy the splendour and respect which it deserves.

On the other hand, the experiences shared in these organizations sometimes protect a Congregation against changes envisaged by a zealous, but perhaps not sufficiently experienced superior, whose view is not broad enough and who may confuse essentials with accidentals. Features which seem outmoded and burdensome may, in fact, be part of the essential sacrifice connected with a particular Institute's apostolate. It would, therefore, be more than simple change to do away with these features.

Since the religious life exists to enable human beings to serve God through other humans, it is only logical that that life should be proportioned to human needs and capacities. It must, therefore, evolve with the evolving times and society, always under the counsel and direction of the Church, which is guided by the Holy Spirit. Healthy change can be a sign of growth, and sound adaptations in a religious Congregation can be a manifestation of that group's eagerness to meet the needs of God's children at a particular time, and a sign that it, too, is one step closer to the establishment of the Kingdom.

Change in the religious life must be effected after a serious consideration of ends and means; it sometimes happens that a Congregation will resist any change, on the conviction that it is remaining loyal to the spirit and aims of its institute. Frequently, however, the loyalty degenerates into a stubborn adhesion to means, while the original ends of the institute are lost sight of. The religious life has always remained essentially the same, while the method of living it has changed down through the centuries. It may be that part of the cause for the lack of vocations in so many Congregations nowadays is due partly to the fact that they live the religious life according to eighteenth- or nineteenth-century ideas, and have, in a way, ceased to keep up with the progress of the Church.

Today's religious must be ready to meet and deal with difficulties which may develop *tomorrow*, not merely the problems that faced their Congregation two or three hundred years ago. As the Church grows and spreads, she needs religious who will adapt themselves, easily and without false scruple, to whatever problems they encounter. The basis of their life must be a strong and dynamic attachment to Christ and the glory of God, so that they are always able to see new ways of praising that glory in any new set of circumstances.

The directives laid down by the General Congress of the States of Perfection in 1951 have been the inspiring force behind many recent adaptations. The directives were aimed at providing every religious with a sufficiently strong cultural, technical and intellectual background, so that he or she would be not merely a powerful spiritual weapon, but a forceful and dynamic social instrument, capable of exercising a proportionate and cogent influence on modern society. At the Congress, every religious group was urged to provide its members with a "specialized and pertinent" technical training, in addition to the usual cultural formation, which would correspond to their particular institute's ends and apostolate. The reason for this recommendation was that apostolic action should constantly adapt itself to the level, abilities, interests and tastes of contemporary men and women, who are the object of every apostolate.

No better conclusion to this chapter can be found than the following extract from a thesis by Don Leoni Aldus on the adaptation and modernization of the religious life for women in Italy:

> Along with an eagerness to increase the number of their convents, especially in underdeveloped areas, religious Congregations of women should also pay close attention to their adaptiveness, so as not to appear old-fashioned to young women, but be able to exhibit that feature of the religious life which should be its most attractive one, namely, the essential superiority of a life of virginity over the married state, and the beauty and excellence, the charm, even, of living in community under the protection of vows of chastity, obedience and poverty. Religious Congregations of women should take care that they are recognized for what they are—families where there is no nostalgia for a natural family, either the one which has been left or the one which will never be established—and thus advertise the fact that a religious family worthy of its name allows its members the fullest possible scope in the cultural and professional fields, to such an extent that they have nothing for which to envy their sisters in the world and may even on this account, should they wish, surpass them.... Finally, a point which cannot be too much emphasized, new vocations must be guarded and guided by a care which is affectionate and spiritually solid, so that the novices may attain to supernatural wisdom, which never excludes from consideration the human talents of mind and heart, nor the need for a pertinent preparation for work undertaken.

These remarks are valid, indeed, far beyond the shores of the Mediterranean and the country for which they were primarily intended.

A P P E N D I X

THE COUNCIL OF MAJOR RELIGIOUS SUPERIORS

In both Great Britain and the U.S.A. there is a Council of Major Religious Superiors. These Councils, one of the developments in the religious life for men and for women in the post-war period, have for object the promotion of the religious life in all its forms. Thus the Council in the United States has six functions: 1. To promote better understanding of the religious life, and to work for the proper religious and apostolic formation of religious. 2. To encourage among religious communities a greater mutual understanding and a more spontaneous mutual assistance. 3. To make the apostolic spirit and work of religious communities more effective. 4. To bring about the closest possible cooperation with the hierarchy. 5. To foster fraternal relations between the religious and the secular clergy and Catholic lay organizations. 6. To represent religious institutes before legitimate authority both ecclesiastical and civil.

In the United States an auxiliary organization of the Council of Major Superiors of Women Religious is the Sister Formation Conference. Its purpose is to advance the spiritual and professional training of sisters. The Conference intends to organize an educational programme for the assistance of sisters from other countries attending juniorates in the United States. Biennial regional programmes in six regions of the United States, cooperation in courses for the training of sisters at the Catholic University of America, Notre Dame and Marquette and the holding of annual conferences for mistresses of postulants, novices and juniors are other means adopted to help forward the training of sisters. A "Sister Formation Bulletin" is published. Conferences for novice mistresses and for superiors on similar lines have been held in England at Spode House in Staffordshire.

SELECT BIBLIOGRAPHY

In this series: CANU, Jean: *Religious Orders of Men*; METZ, René: *What is Canon Law?*; REIDY, Gabriel, O.F.M.: *Secular Institutes.*

ANSON, Peter F.: *The Religious Orders and Congregations of Great Britain and Ireland,* Worcester, Stanbrook Abbey, 1949.

AUCLAIR, Marcelle: *St Teresa of Avila,* New York, Pantheon, and London, Burns and Oates, 1953.

BENEDICTINES of Stanbrook: *In a Great Tradition,* London, Murray, 1956.

BOUYER, Louis: *The Meaning of the Monastic Life,* New York, Kenedy, and London, Burns and Oates, 1955.

CREUSEN, J., S.J.: *Religious Men and Women in the Code,* revised edn, Milwaukee, Bruce, 1953.

FARRELL, Edward, O.P.: *Theology of Religious Vocation,* St Louis, Mo., Herder, 1951.

HARTDEGAN, Stephen, O.F.M., and Sister M. WINEFRIDE, S.A.C.: *Secular Institutes in the United States, Religious Life in the United States,* Proceedings of National Congress of Religious, 1952, 2 volumes, New York, Paulist Press, 1952.

MARY LAURENCE, Sister, O.P.: *The Convent and the World,* Westminster, Md, Newman Press, 1954.

McCARTHY, Thomas P.: *Guide to the Catholic Sisterhoods in the United States,* Washington, Catholic Univ. Press, 1955.

O'LEARY, Mary: *Our Time is Now: A Study of Some Modern Congregations and Secular Institutes,* Westminster, Md, Newman Press, and London, Burns and Oates, 1955.

POURRAT, Pierre: *Christian Spirituality,* volumes I–III, London, Burns and Oates, 1922–4, and volumes I–IV, Westminster, Md, Newman Press, 1953–8.

SHEPPARD, L. C.: *Barbe Acarie, Wife and Mystic,* New York, McKay, and London, Burns and Oates, 1953.